I0101118

Eclipse of Rules
© Dale Hoagland, 2017

All rights reserved. No part of this book may be reproduced or transmitted in any form without written permission from the publisher, except by a reviewer who may quote brief passages for review purposes. If you are reading this book and did not buy it or win it in a contest by the author, publisher, or authorized distributor, you are reading an illegal copy. This hurts the author and publisher. Please delete and purchase a legal copy from one of its distributors.

Printed in The United States of America

DEDICATION

To the law enforcement men and women who risk it all.

ECLIPSE OF RULES

By Dale Hoagland

LOVE AT FIRST SIGHT

Cam knew he was an asshole, but he didn't need some snot nosed rookie who wasn't even off probation yet telling him so. There were unwritten rules in police work and rule number one was that rookies should shut up and show a little respect for veterans. There was always a price to be paid when they didn't. The cost for Officer Sanchez today was that his patrol car was going to get sabotaged in a major way.

Sanchez's passing comment ("what an asshole") at shift briefing was in response to Cam saying that "technology was not a substitute for good police work." Cam also added that all these new recruits acted just like crack addicts when it came to their cell phones. Earlier that week, the rookie had his nose in his MDT (mobile data terminal/in car computer) when he should have been watching the driver on a traffic stop. The driver drove away while the rookie was typing.

Cam was watching Sanchez make yet another mistake by leaving his patrol car unlocked at a call where he was taking a vandalism report. That was a dumb move for a number of reasons. Not only is it possible to get equipment stolen, like shotguns, ticket books etc. but it's a good way to get your car trashed. Several years ago, a patrol officer made this error and a group of gang bangers who happened to be strolling down the street pissed inside his car, literally soaking every square inch of the front seat.

Today's lesson would not be quite so unsanitary but it would make a couple of things crystal clear: lock your patrol car and don't fuck with Cam.

Cam's partner Bobby watched as Cam slid out of his marked unit and into Sanchez's, where he pushed the A/C fan switch to high, then sprayed pepper spray in both air conditioning vents located on either side of the steering wheel. He directed the driver's side ducts so they vented right at the driver. He then turned on all the lights and sirens full blast so that when the ignition was activated they'd be in full operation along with the A/C. He also turned up the police radio and the car radio to full volume which was guaranteed to blow the rookie's ear ballast. Due to the heavy battery drain of police hardware none of this equipment would be active till he started the engine, but once it was turned over, stand by for the fun.

On a warm summer day like this when the bright sun reflected off of the patrol car windows it was a given that the inside of a car with air conditioning was the place to be, so Officer Sanchez's car seemed to be calling to him. Dark blue uniforms with body armor underneath made all cops want back in their car on summer days.

When Cam returned to his car, Bobby said, "Cam, is this absolutely necessary?"

Bobby had been witness to more than enough of these juvenile pranks.

"Yes, this smart mouthed little shit has to learn some respect. Now, we'll just park across the street and watch the fun."

As Officer Sanchez walked to his car on this bright July day, he was a picture of professionalism. He surveyed his surroundings with a quick look to the left than right. His blue uniform was tailored, his shoes were shined and the sunglasses he so carefully slid into place were expensive. His hair was trimmed high and tight and he observed all the tactical awareness appropriate for a cop in uniform. He sat down in his unit, shut the door, buckled up and fired it up so he could notify dispatch that he was back in service. Then all hell broke loose. He instantly got a snoot full of pepper spray and the noise was deafening. All five of his senses where under direct attack. In his panic, he couldn't decide whether to get out of the car and run, or attack all the mutinous equipment. He went so far as to get his seat belt off, open the car door and get one foot on the ground but then decided he had to get all the sirens and radios quieted before it started to draw a crowd. His hands were slapping switches and knobs while he cried, choked, and blinked, eventually shutting down the chaos. He stepped out of the car to try to get some fresh air and his bearings when it fully sunk in that this was an act of revenge and training from his "friends." He almost thought he could see two cops driving away laughing their heads off, but he couldn't be sure because he was not seeing too well at the moment. Sometimes the most memorable training is slightly painful. Cops would often "ambush" one another with pranks not only because it was fun but also as a message to stay sharp. There are people out there that want to hurt you.

Technology was changing law enforcement as fast as it was changing every other aspect of human existence. The new rookies were relying on it to save them from death or injury and that was a huge mistake. The technology could help you be a better investigator or more efficient but it wasn't a substitute for good old-fashioned survival skills.

Many of the training officers would start training with new rookies by telling them, "Turn off the MDT and your cell phone. They won't stop bullets." Once they learned that awareness and tactics, not gadgets, make you safe, they were allowed to add the electronics. Sometimes it took weeks or months before the technology was added to the training. Bobby was known on the department as a tech savant but was also respected because he knew the limits of its value in all aspects of his life.

∞

If Officer Sanchez had asked anybody he worked with they would have told him, "Don't fuck with CAM." Cameron Addison Michaelson (his mother loved acronyms) was raised tough. Time and police work only made him tougher. Cam came from a big family in Sacramento California's Central Valley, with two older brothers who thought it was their job to make their little brother hard and resilient. In other words, they tortured the poor boy with every ornery trick that brothers ever played on one another. He grew up on the poor side of town with a dad who worked his ass off and a mother who demanded that the boys become literate. She pushed college, the arts, and all things intellectual and cultured. His dad had only one request for Cam's education. That he be allowed to take karate lessons. Dad reasoned that Cam's bad temper and boundless energy needed an outlet. He also thought Cam needed some relief from his mother's "cultural training." The boys hated mom's attempt to elevate their intellects and dad thought it was funny. The result in Cam's case was a 6-foot 2-inch, 195 lb. jock who could kick a crook's ass while giving him a lecture about the meaning of life "ala Nietzsche." By age 14 after 7 years of karate training his older brothers learned that if they wanted to mess with Cam they needed to be quick and not get cornered by him or they might get hurt.

Much to his mother's discomfort all this education and reading made Cam smart, irreverent and a stone-cold atheist with a biting intellectual tongue. His irreverence was legendary in the family and stories of how he was asked to stop attending Sunday school at his mother's church were often repeated at holiday dinners. Apparently rude questions about biblical logic put to the Sunday school teacher were not welcome on the path to enlightenment. Fate, along with one life-altering moment of violence, made him dangerously decisive. People who didn't know him well were often startled by a penetrating stare from his deep dark eyes framed by his jet-black hair. His karate instructor, a half Japanese and half black man with a sardonic wit, would sometimes describe Cam as "black lightning."

Because of Cam's magnetic personality some genius on the third floor with bars on his collar decided that he should be partnered up with Bobby. The management's theory being that their vastly different views of the world would moderate each other's personality. It so far, wasn't working. Bobby's positive attitude and pleasant personality only served to irritate Cam and Bobby was wondering what he'd done to the police administration that warranted such punishment. He'd been a San Jose cop for about six years and often wondered about management's thought process, but this one actually made him angry. Bobby wasn't exactly the polar opposite of Cam but he was enough of an opposite that the sight of the two partners together made other cops smile and shake their heads.

Bobby Wright was the oldest of seven children born to Mormon farmers. His senior year at Gilroy high school found him as tall as he was ever going to get at 5 feet 9 and he lettered in two sports, football and wrestling. He wrestled in the 175 lbs. weight category and was rock hard. Nothing had changed much since then because he worked out like a maniac and volunteered at the local high school as an assistant wrestling coach. He kept his skills honed by wrestling with the varsity seniors who outweighed him by 30 lbs. He was always the caretaker and peacemaker of his brothers and sisters. His deep blue eyes, disarming smile and sandy colored hair painted the perfect picture of a gentle soul. Being basically a nice guy, he didn't like the violence that was an inherent part of law enforcement, but when needed, he could tie crooks in a knot in seconds using one of his extremely painful wrestling holds. Suspects who experienced this seldom figured out how they ended up in such an incapacitated state so quickly.

His training officer liked to say, "Piss off Bobby and he'll show an asshole his own asshole."

The first time Bobby ever left home for more than a night was to do his mission service at a church in Mexico. It was then, as a teenager, that he decided he wanted to be a cop.

He had gone down to a public park where teens were having a dance and watched the fear and anxious behavior by the Mexican families when the police showed up to a disturbance. He decided then, that people had a right to trust their law enforcement officers. Even after six years on the job he believed in the "Peace Officer Code of Ethics," just as strongly as the day he raised his right hand and recited it at his academy graduation.

∞

Their first call of the swing shift, which was 2:00 pm till midnight with the ten-hour shifts, was a cold burglary. The burglary was cold but the weather was not. It was summer and that meant more rip offs because that's when decent citizens took their vacations and became one of the over 5,000 burglary victims every year in the city. Usually day shift got to take all of these reports because folks would come back from vacation late Sunday night and discover that some piece of shit stole all their stuff while they were out of town. They generally waited till the next morning to call it in, assuming correctly that not much could be done. This one was slightly different because it was a day time rip off while the victims were at work. A call like this would normally be handled on line or by civilian department employees because it wasn't a hot call or something that really involved a need for a guy with a gun but all the CSO's (community service officers) were tied up on other long calls and the sergeant wanted this one handled now. Apparently, the homeowner knew someone who knew someone in city government. This instantly irritated Cam.

"Politics can contaminate everything it touches, you know that?"

Bobby said, "Ya, but that's okay. We weren't doing much anyway."

As they rolled up to the call Bobby got out and talked with the homeowner as he started a report. Cam looked around the scene and asked a few questions.

"I'm so God damn sick of 'Entry, Exit, Prowl and MO (method of operation) on these burglaries I could puke, they're all the same with no hope and no suspects," Cam said. "I really need to trade in this uniform for some plain clothes."

All the rip off reports were the same, just different victims, houses and times. Drug addicts were making it so decent citizens had to live in fortified jails while dopers ran free. Half the houses in the city were decorated with alarms and bars on the windows and doors. Dogs and guns were the second line of defense. This victim had been ripped off before and hadn't even replaced all the stuff he'd lost last time.

Many officers started their reports by asking, "When was the last time you were hit? Which of your neighbors are on parole or probation?" Cam's first impression of this neighborhood was that it was headed downhill. Houses were being fitted with window and door bars and some landscape architect had built a Virgin of Guadalupe statue in the front yard.

Cam loved old time rock and roll mainly because it was frowned upon by his mom, and this rip off reminded him of Janis's line, "Freedom's just another word for nothing left to lose." As he sang the words, Bobby and the victim both failed to find the amusement in this musical attempt at philosophy. Bobby retrieved a blank property form and told the victim to list specific information about the stolen property, like serial numbers, makes and models, and he'd get it listed in the stolen property computer.

"We might find it at a search warrant or flea market."

When Bobby and Cam got back in their patrol car Cam said, "Why did you lie to the guy like that Bobby? You'll give him false hope."

Bobby said, "It could happen. It does happen every once and a while."

This made Cam just shake his head and break into a chorus of, "It's a beautiful day in the neighborhood, won't you be my neighbor?"

As Bobby glanced over at Cam's smart-ass smirk he thought to himself, "The rookie was dead-on right about Cam."

∞

Not all the calls they took that day were as easy and routine as a cold burglary. Later that day, they were dispatched to the local hospital, an ultra-modern glass and steel mega-building, to see the admitting nurse in the emergency room. Cops and nurses knew each other well. Cops were always in ERs with victims or arresting loaded crazies. After a while they shared stories, bad hours, coffee and occasional beds.

When they arrived, the head nurse told Cam and Bobby that she'd just admitted a 22-year-old black female with multiple broken facial bones, bruises all over her body, missing patches of hair and evidence of a severe sexual assault, vaginally and rectally. The nurse believed, from previous medical contact, that the girl was a gang prostitute.

With obvious rage in her voice she said, "They slowed down by the front door of the ER and threw her out of the car like she was so much trash. Those bastards should all burn in hell."

The security guards that are required in all California emergency rooms were dealing with another victim of drug abuse and his family so there was no description of the vehicle that dumped her.

When Bobby and Cam entered her room, she was lying in bed with tubes in her arms and monitors displaying her vitals. Her badly bruised face was bandaged and Cam thought to himself that he'd seen auto accident victims that looked like this. Bobby introduced himself and Cam to the girl and found out her name was Dawn. Dawn was a thin 22-year-old black and Asian girl with a short natural and what had been a striking face. She had light blue eyes which seemed wrong somehow, but beautiful none the less.

When Bobby asked her, "What happened to you?" he didn't get a response at first. He just quietly sat at the foot of her bed and said, "That's fine if you don't feel like talking, Dawn. My partner and I just started our shift and we still have nine hours to go, so we can hang with you a while until you feel better and want to talk." Bobby pulled out a report form from his clip board, and started to write. Cam found a magazine on a cabinet in the room and started to flip through the pages as he navigated toward a chair in the corner. Cam recognized Bobby's tactic. He knew that Bobby had no intention of spending over a few minutes with this girl but that reluctant victims like this wanted the cops to go away and once they realized that they weren't going away, would give out enough information to satisfy the officers. A few minutes went by and as they listened to all the hospital machines and apparatus that hummed its constant background noise, Bobby thought, "This is probably the first time in years that Dawn has been in a place where she wasn't terrified of violence."

Dawn eventually said, "Look, I can't talk to you about this because if I do it'll cause me more grief. Let's just say I had a problem with my boss and he had some of his people talk with me. It was my fault. I fucked up." She winced as she talked because the slightest facial movements pulled stiches.

As Bobby was trying to pry some details out of her, like when and where all this happened, Cam handed him a receipt for a prostitution bail arrest. While Bobby had been talking with Dawn, Cam was conducting a little off the record search of Dawn's purse that he'd found in the lower drawer of the cabinet. Cam figured an illegal search is only a problem if you're trying to get something admitted into evidence in court. The rest of the time it was just good investigative work.

When he read the name of who posted the bail on the receipt Bobby nodded and said, "Dawn, the guy who ordered your beating won't happen to be J-Tra, would it?"

Dawn looked down in a moment of fear, and said, "I ain't saying shit. You guys'll get me killed."

Bobby stood up and said, "Dawn, we can't help you if you won't work with us. We can relocate you and give you protection but it's in your hands." Dawn closed her eyes and rolled away from Bobby in the bed turning her back to him. The conversation was over.

Cam walked over to the bedside table and placed Dawn's leather purse on top of it. He pulled a business card out of his wallet and as she watched he slid the card in her purse. With a stone-cold stare, Cam made eye contact with Dawn and he saw that she locked eyes with him, "I'm tougher than that punk, Dawn. I can protect you." He nodded and left her room.

As Cam and Bobby walked out of the hospital and got into their marked unit Bobby said, "Another victim of the infamous Mr. J-Tra."

Cam's temper was at a boiling point Bobby seldom saw.

"I'm telling you Bobby, that son of a bitch is going down. I don't care what it takes or how long, he's fucking going down."

Bobby was writing on the report when he admonished Cam, "You know that good cops don't get personally invested in these kinds of situations. It will eat you up if you let it. How many good cops do you know that are haunted by the case they couldn't close?"

Cam said, "I know. You're right. I'll try to rise above it but I do now have a new career goal in my sights. That asshole J-Tra has his own personal cop who will give him more law enforcement services than he ever thought possible."

After a few years on the job most officers became institutionalized. They became slightly numbed to the legal system, allowing thugs like J-Tra to operate just outside the grasp of the law. It became a game where guilt was not an issue, the issue was whether you caught the crook "fairly." When you went to court, often everyone in the courtroom - judge, attorneys, clerks, bailiffs and spectators - knew the crook was guilty. The whole point in being there was just to make sure the cops played by the rules.

Everyone who worked in this system understood search and seizure and how important due process was to constitutional rights, but it seemed as though victims were forgotten in this legal theory. One person's constitutional right was another person's misery. Many years ago, the courts decided that the solution to police misconduct during searches or interrogations was to throw out the tainted evidence, but it really didn't punish the officers. It punished the public. Most officers adjusted to the rules of the game and became numb to its unfairness and illogic. Cam never was quite able to compartmentalize the theory without looking at the victim.

Dawn's story wasn't unique. Her family was poor and her father nonexistent. Her mother worked all day and pulled overtime shifts some evenings cleaning commercial buildings for a maintenance contractor. Dawn helped supervise her three brothers, or at least tried. At 15 it was hard to get her 14 and 12-year-old brothers to mind her. The 8-year-old would listen but not for long. The street was too strong a call and the older boys would sneak out when she wasn't looking. Respect for women was hard to find in the ghetto, and her mother's threats only worked for a while.

When Raphael started to call her, and meet her in front of her house with an ice cream cone, she was smitten. No male of any age had ever treated her politely or bought her anything. She craved the attention and dreamed of a knight in shining armor to take her away from her crappy life. It was the general hopelessness of her existence that was dragging her down. She wouldn't get to go to college and her brothers were on the thug path. She wanted to escape and a lie was easy to buy, especially if it was from a sweet talking handsome guy.

Raphael knew his business. When you recruit for the gang you don't get attached to the women you target. You remember that very soon they'll be whores and junkies so the rule is: date them, drug them, pimp them and move on. He started to spend a lot of time with Dawn and took her on expensive dates. He introduced her to new exciting people, some of whom scared her but Raphael was always there to protect her so she felt safe. He seemed to be in control of everything and made her feel that. As long as he was there nothing bad could happen. The fact that he was three years older than her didn't scare her because he was so attentive and gentle. He was actually eight years older than she was, but she didn't know that until months later, after it was already too late. When she was first introduced to dope she tried to say no but the pressure was intense from Raphael and his friends. Her self-esteem wasn't up to the continual bombardment and the thought of losing him meant a return to her hopeless existence. She felt it would suffocate her as it did her mother. So, she caved.

Many people debate whether or not marijuana is a "gateway" drug, but one thing is for sure, addicts don't start out their drug experience by fixing heroin. The mindset is what's important. Once you've made up your mind to use an illegal substance to get loaded, it doesn't take much to take the next step to a higher high. Many people confuse a substance problem with a behavior problem. A lot of people never take that escapist route, but many with problems do. She took the first step, and then the next, and before she knew what was happening Raphael and she were partying with the heavyweights. The sex came in tandem with the drugs. Her inhibitions were down when she was loaded and she wasn't fit to take care of herself. The contemporary "consent" philosophy that is so heavily stressed on college campuses is laughed at on the street.

Every lowlife knew, "That's what drugs and booze are for, to get a woman loaded so you can fuck her."

Dawn was loaned out to other junior gang members and when she protested and cried Raphael showed her his other side. He slapped her bloody and introduced her to another more humiliating way to have sex. The message was clear, cry all you want but this is your new life. Eventually she was the gang's "party girl" and when they were tired of her she was turned out to do street work. If she wanted to get her twice a day fix she had to play ball. Many times she thought about running away or committing suicide, but she never could quite get it done. The dope kept pulling her back. As long as addicts were using, all the exit ramps that you would have used in your former life seemed unrealistic.

Cam and Bobby knew the story inside and out. It's an old one that repeats itself over and over again.

∞

After a few car stops and suspicious persons calls it was time to eat. Cam was a modified health nut and while he would eat "junk food" on rare occasions, he normally packed a small ice chest with some healthier food than you could get in a drive through. His view of food was that it was fuel for his karate and exercise. Bad fuel was a handicap. With an occasional exception neither officer liked to go into a restaurant because people wouldn't leave you alone. Someone was always parking their butt in front of your booth telling you about the bullshit ticket they got or complaining about that their brother in law was getting harassed by the cops. Even if they were there to tell you about how they loved police, they were still "there." Bobby used to get fast food but Cam gave him so much crap about what was really in that stuff that Bobby gave up and started packing his lunch also. Cam really convinced Bobby when he asked the country boy what hogs ate on the farm and then read him research from Eric Schlosser's classic book *Fast Food Nation*. The similarity to processed foods was uncomfortably close.

They found a park on their beat that was large and generally unused due to the gang bangers hanging out there. They jumped the curb with the patrol car, drove across the lawn and found a knoll to set atop while they ate. They could eat without being bothered, chase off a few dirt bags, and get a little evening breeze coming through their patrol car doors that were propped open. It was always the same scene. When they showed up low riders and customized Hondas would slowly decide to leave. The loud rap music would drive away along with bobbing heads and frowning homeboys.

When Cam asked Bobby how the kids were doing, Bobby said, "It's time to put my daughter in school and I'm thinking about a charter religious school that my church uses. The problem is that it cost a hunk of change."

Cam happened to be eating an apple which reminded him of the biblical story of Adam and Eve. "So, I guess the only question is, do you want someone teaching your kid that the universe is only 6,000 years old or 14 billion years old?" As Cam took another noisy bite out of his crisp apple he grinned at Bobby's discomfort.

Bobby said, "I don't think it's impossible to believe in the Bible and science at the same time."

Cam laughed and said, "Nope, half the population of this great country does, but a smart guy like you should be intellectually brave and reconcile the discrepancy in the facts because we both know that they both can't be true."

Bobby having covered this ground before, decided to change the subject so he asked Cam if he'd seen the openings notice for the Gang Unit and Cam said, "Ya, you thinking about doing it, Bobby?"

"It's time you know. I've pushed around this patrol car for a few years and I need to do something to juice up my resume."

Cam nodded, "I already put in for it, mostly because I'm bored shitless with this assignment and would like a little more freedom to make cases on real heavyweight crooks."

Bobby looked at Cam and with a big smile on his face. "You know, we'd be a logical replacement for one of the two-man teams they have open and we both have a lot of seniority compared to most of the other street dogs. They just might pick both of us and make us partners on the gang unit." Cam grimaced as he looked at Bobby and they both started to laugh. Cam thought, "I could do worse than this hallelujah hero, but a change might be nice too."

KEEP THEM GUESSING

Just as they were finishing up their meal the MDT beeped at them that they had a call. An elderly man was reporting the death of his wife at their residence. Dispatch said this was a cold call and was apparently natural causes. As a result of all the layoffs and budget cuts, it would be up to them, the investigating officers, to decide whether the homicide detectives needed to be called, or just the coroner.

Cam said, "Crap, why do these calls always come in when I have a full stomach. I hope to Christ she's fresh and hasn't lost her cookies." Like a lot of veterans who were experienced at handling dead body calls, especially aged dead bodies, he kept a jar of Menthol Ointment in his equipment bag that he could smear under his nose or on a bandana tied over his mouth and nose, so the smell didn't gag him when he went in the house. It seemed like no matter how much you washed or blew your nose the dead body odor took forever to go away. The department shrinks said it was a mental memory but whatever it was it still smelled bad. They'd had a string of 90-degree days and it didn't take long at that temperature to ripen a body.

The last homicide they had investigated two months ago turned out to be in a neighboring jurisdiction. That time they were dispatched to a rural edge of town on a reported woman lying in the bushes. Two other units were also dispatched because it was a problem area with lots of homeless people, drug addicts, and crime. Cam and Bobby weren't the assigned primary unit, but they were the first to arrive at the scene. Cam knew instantly that this ripe corpse laying amongst the trash, wrecked shopping carts and booze bottles would be handed over to the Sheriff's Office because it was just outside the city limits, so as he waited for the other assigned beat unit he wrote a little note for the lead detective from the S.O. This detective was a famous mad dog. He would scream and yell and generally throw a conniption if one thing was disturbed at a crime scene, even if it involved officer safety, like securing a gun. The note read, "Officer Richards, these city guys didn't move or touch anything at your crime scene. Signed, Dead Lady." Then Cam lifted the dead lady's arm and put the folded note in the arm pit before lowering the arm.

They found that this current death wasn't as unpleasant, because it was fresh. The woman had died in the night and the husband had sat with her all day before he finally was ready to call the police and have her taken away. Bobby didn't even need to check her vitals as rigor and lividity (the blood had drained to the lowest area of her body) had already set in. Death was obvious. Cam started to talk with the husband and, for once in his life, was gentle and polite. The old guy, Thomas White, was a military vet with 30 years of service in the U.S. Army and he and his wife were childhood sweethearts. They had a couple of kids who lived out of state that didn't make it home often. As Cam talked with the husband in this 1940's craftsman cottage that reminded him of his parents first home, Bobby looked through the medication on a knitted doily covering the bed stand. The place was 15 degrees too hot and smelled musty like a lot of older folks' homes. To quote Cam's little sister, "It smelled like vitamins and farts." The nightstand looked like a drug store annex and the specific medications drew a picture of a very sick woman. Bobby joined the other two men in the living room and asked the husband about his wives' illnesses.

Mr. White explained, "My wife had multiple conditions that made her life a living hell. She had congestive heart failure, scoliosis, diabetes, and was just diagnosed with Alzheimer's. We spent the majority of our free time at doctor's offices getting tests and waiting to see specialists. The doctor had given her methadone for the scoliosis back pain because her vertebrae were literally crumbling." Mr. White explained that they had talked about the demeaning loss of intellectual control that comes with Alzheimer's and her constant pain that could only be controlled with the Methadone, which made her sleep through the day. He said she begged him to help her end her life on her terms, so she could be free of the pain and the fear.

He said, "This wasn't the first time we had had this conversation but I was usually able to put it off and stall her until this time. I finally agreed after she explained that this was about her, not me, and that I would have to deal with my own loneliness because this was something I needed to do for her."

They decided to listen to some nice music, talk, drink a couple of bottles of good wine and she would take fatal amounts of two different prescription pain pills. The OxyContin was left over from some oral surgery she had two years ago and the Fentanyl was prescribed originally for the back pain till it was found to be too strong. Either one alone was dangerous, but both when combined with the Methadone and wine were lethal. She wasn't able to function too well after the wine, so he had helped her get all the pills down. They did their job after a couple of hours, so he just sat with her all night holding her hand and crying.

Often, when spouses like Mr. White realized that their control over events had ended and someone's death had altered their life, many thoughts competed for attention. There's the struggle with the loss and loneliness that comes with losing a lifetime partner, but also a sense of relief in not having to care for a very ill loved one which, of course, makes for wholesale guilt.

Well into the next day, after he'd worked through some of his grief, Mr. White called the dispatcher and then was faced with actually losing his wife's body forever. Death was so damn final and absolutely non-negotiable. He told Cam that he'd lost many friends and fellow soldiers throughout his life, but nothing prepared him for this. He couldn't ever remember being without her.

Cam notified the coroner and the mortuary while he wrote his report. After the mortuary came for the body and left, Mr. White sat on the couch and felt hollow, as if he couldn't catch his breath. Mr. White had never felt like this in his life.

Cam filled out the rest of the report and listed the investigative cause of death to be accidental overdose and medical complication in a very ill woman. The autopsy would give the final cause of death but for now there would be no arrest or investigation. Cam knew that the detectives were so overloaded with real homicides, that when a beat cop with 8 years' experience said there wasn't a crime they were glad to file it and move on.

Bobby asked Cam to step into the kitchen for a moment. "Cam, are you sure about this? This is an assisted suicide and while this guy is no Jack Kevorkian, he did kill his wife."

"Ya, I know Bobby, but I didn't become a cop to put guys like this in jail. You were doing the dead body piece of the investigation, so let me take the heat for the old man's statement. If things turn to shit it will be my problem."

Bobby nodded his head and said, "Okay, but I am concerned about this uncharacteristic display of compassion from you. You feel alright?"

Cam leaned forward and whispered in Bobby's ear, "Fuck you Bobby."

Bobby smiled at Cam's irritation, nudged him with his shoulder and went back into the bedroom.

While Bobby bagged up the medication for autopsy reference, Cam told the old guy, "I'm going to write this up as an accidental overdose." Mr. White was old and couldn't hear well but he was as sharp as anybody half his age. He fully understood what Cam was doing. Cam explained, "If you start feeling a need to confess, you need to talk to a priest, not your kids or anyone else. I could get in a lot of trouble if you started talking about this."

Mr. White said, "I understand, I've no one to talk with anyway."

Cam thought to himself, if the old guy started jawing, most people will write it off as senile babbling and if push comes to shove, "He never told me that." Who would believe Cam showed compassion anyway?

Cam gave Mr. White his personal cell phone number and told him to call if he had any questions or problems. This was highly unusual because cops normally give out the station number so citizens don't have access to their personal phone. Bobby wasn't sure if it was compassion or butt covering. He thought it might be a little of both.

∞

Unusual wasn't that unusual with Cam. He was always bending rules and being dangerously creative.

About a year ago the partners were walking through a bar around 11:00 pm, just doing a routine bar check for problems when they happened to encounter a drunk trying to get his car out of a rear alley parking space. The guy was in his mid-fifties with a beer belly and some strange liquid plastering down his hair. He was so hammered he'd hit a row of trash dumpsters and couldn't find a forward gear. Bobby reached through the driver's window and killed the ignition. They pulled him out of the car for a field sobriety check and he reeked of alcohol. As he was failing the test and about to be cuffed and transported, an emergency call came across their radio. A group of officers at a county fair low rider car show found themselves in the middle of a full-blown riot. They had put out an 11-99 call which essentially means every cop in radio broadcast distance was supposed to respond code 3.

Bobby remembered looking at Cam and saying, "Crap, what are going to do with him?" Knowing that they could not respond with a prisoner in the car because of liability nor could they let this guy get behind the wheel again, they had a problem.

Cam took the guy's car keys and told him, "Watch this." He threw the car keys on the top of the bar's roof, which was a 20-foot flat top.

He told Bobby, "Come on. If he can get those he's sober." As they drove away the drunk sat down in the alley and stared forlornly at the roof.

Bobby said, "Hope he doesn't file a complaint."

Cam laughed, "Who'd believe a story like that from a drunk? Here's the first rule in breaking rules, Bobby: make your conduct so bizarre it lacks credibility on its face." There were occasions when Bobby didn't know whether to laugh or fear for his job.

Bobby had discovered over the last several years that Cam was not afraid of making decisions. Sometimes it was almost frightening how he could make a split-second decision in which life, death, freedom, litigation, and the general well-being of multiple people were at stake. What Bobby didn't fully understand, in the beginning, was that these decisions weren't made lightly. Cam just believed that his job was to make tough decisions, because he wasn't hired to be a pussy and think things to death. He knew that he would occasionally make a mistake, but that was the price of doing police business. Indecisiveness was the real danger in street work. That got people hurt. There were times to go with the flow and times to make things flow a specific direction. Several times when they were in serious danger he did the most outrageous, violent thing he could think of and it worked because it was so unexpected.

For example, one night two years ago, when they were responding to an address just west of Diablo St., a crazy, drunk, suicidal excon started shooting at their patrol car as they arrived at his house. The entire call was a fake disturbance designed to ambush the officers responding. The excon was standing on a raised front porch between two pillars aiming his rifle at them as they rounded the corner driving toward him. Cam figured they wouldn't survive an attack with an AR15 assault rifle by trying to drive past the shooter so he screamed at Bobby to lay down on the front seat as he punched the gas pedal, driving the patrol unit directly at the shooter, across the front lawn and up the steps on to the front porch, sending the shooter into his living room the hard way.

He later told the patrol Sergeant he believed that, "The engine block was better at stopping bullets than the door panel." He brought down the porch, half the living room, sent the shooter to the hospital, and totaled a patrol car. It made for one dramatic front-page newspaper picture. Cam's actions that night saved their lives.

∞

Cam learned early in life that being timid didn't pay. The lesson he learned in karate at a very young age was, to pay attention to the threat, let others' emotions work in your favor, and when you strike make it count. All his life experience reinforced that lesson, especially one incident on a cool afternoon in October when he had just turned 17.

Cam's father had quite literally worked himself to death. He had a heart attack while lifting a heavy piece of machinery at his manufacturing plant job. Cam's memories of his father were virtually all good ones. His dad usually had a smile on his face and seldom issued a harsh comment. Cam's dad and mom were embarrassingly affectionate, which made for secure children even if they did roll their eyes at their parents' old-fashioned hand holding. Cam often thought about his dad's huge bear hugs. While he never said, "I love you," the message was unmistakable. His dad would grab all the kids one at a time and hug them into his strong chest and hold them for a few seconds. When he would release them, he'd put his big hands on either side of their head and give them a big kiss right on their forehead. He'd look them directly in the eye and smile till they smiled back, then he'd turn them loose. Cam's little sister had started to do the same routine to her father, which always made him break out a big belly laugh.

His dad's death had hit the family like a sledge hammer between the shoulder blades and left them without a major wage earner, so even though there was a modest insurance policy on his dad, his mother began working as a clerk in a neighborhood grocery store. Cam's two older brothers were away at college and almost done so his mom made them swear to finish school and not waste all their dad's effort to get them an education. This created some financial pressure on the family but Cam's mom was determined to get all the kids through college at any cost. Cam's little sister was still at home and starting high school with Cam just getting ready to finish, so it was just the two of them living with Mom.

As if life hadn't thrown the family enough of a curve, after several months of widowhood his mother started dating an old friend of his dad's. After a several more months of dating, Cam's mother got married. She believed it would be best for the kids to have a real family and needed help with the expenses. She was wrong, it wasn't good at all for the family.

Cam hated the guy, but he kept his mouth shut because he knew that loneliness was everything it was cracked up to be and he knew the responsibilities his mother had were oppressive. He figured that he wasn't going to live at home much longer and he could just stay gone most of the time till he moved out. This was a good plan but, like most good plans, reality intruded and it was quickly thrown onto the scrap heap.

The new stepdad may have been a friend of Cam's dad, but Cam doubted he'd have sanctioned a marriage with the guy. He had a drinking problem and when he drank he got mean. The fights behind closed doors began to increase and Cam had several heart to heart talks with his mother about ending the marriage, but she just didn't want to fail. She thought it was her responsibility to make it work and, like many naive women, thought that love would make the guy come around. She should have been tipped off to what lay in the future when the pushing, shoving, and threats of violence started to surface, but she was truly like the frog in the hot water. She didn't notice that boiling occurs a degree at a time. After one particularly ugly night of arguing, Cam came home to find his mother crying with a big dark bruise on her check and a split lip. His rage was uncontrollable and it took all night and all her influence over Cam to stop him from using his martial arts training to hospitalize the bully. Cam's mother was so frightened for the stepdad's safety she told him to stay away for a couple of days till Cam cooled down.

She said, "I can't guarantee what Cam will do and I'm scared to death he'll be so crazy that he might kill you." When the bully returned home two days later Cam cornered him in the garage and told him if he ever touched his mother again he would kill him. When the bully laughed at him, Cam executed a karate kick two inches from the guy's chest that left a dent 6" deep in the side of his pickup truck.

Cam pointed at it and said, "That's what your head's going to look like, Cocksucker, if you ever touch her again." The step father was visibly frightened and retreated into the house. When he looked in Cam's deep black eyes he saw a primal rage that made him lose his breath.

Things remained quiet for about a month till the honeymoon cycle of domestic violence was over and the inevitable escalation started again. One Saturday afternoon Cam was at his best friend's house a few houses down the block in this modest working-class neighborhood.

Jimmy Scallon was two years older than Cam but they were tight as two guys could be. They had gone to school together and took karate lessons at the same studio. All the neighborhood kids, including Cam's brothers and Jimmy's, would get together on summer evenings for a game of softball on a vacant lot on their street. After Cam's brothers left for college, Jimmy was the only one he could talk with about his home situation.

As Cam left Jimmy's and arrived home he noticed his little sister crying on the brick front porch leaning against a support post.

When Cam approached he looked at her and said, "What?"

All she said, while hugging her pet cat was, "He's at it again."

Cam pulled open the screen door, stepped inside to the sound of the bully screaming, "You fucking bitch!" and the sound of a aluminum baseball bat hitting his mother. The hollow ring of an aluminum bat echoed off the stucco walls. As he ran down the hard wood floor hallway to the back of the house he could see his mother lying on the bedroom floor with blood running from her head, splattered on the white sheetrock walls and floor. The bully was holding the bat in one hand staring down at her in a drunken rage.

Cam screamed at him, "Stop" and as the thug turned he swung the bat at Cam's head with as much force as he could. Cam was able to side step into the bathroom directly across the hall from the bedroom, as the bat hit the door casing, barely missing Cam's head and leaving a 3" dent in the wood. The bully stepped forward with a two-handed grip to swing the bat again when Cam, in a split-second decision, picked up a small screw driver that was left lying on the counter after someone was using it to repair drawer handles and with a lightning quick move stabbed the bully with an upward motion in the stomach right under the sternum. The screw driver only had a 4" shank and it didn't penetrate far enough to stop a raging drunk. It only angered him. Cam knew from all his martial arts training that the most dangerous thing alive was an angry wounded animal so necessity required him to act quickly. It took him only 2 seconds to decide on his next tactical move. He delivered a standard martial arts jab with an open palm to the butt of the screw driver. He aimed his palm directly at the yellow plastic handle butt. The karate mantra was "punch through the target, not at it." He had punched blocking dummies and pads at least a million times in gym practice and the motion that delivered tremendous force was as naturally as breathing. The additional three inches of handle was driven up and into the chest far enough to reach the heart. The shocked look on the bully's face told Cam everything he needed to know. A dynamic violent encounter now shifted in a split second to an almost frozen moment of shock and disbelief. The abuser was five seconds from being dead.

As the bully dropped to his knees with an astonished look on his face, Cam leaned forward and said quietly into his ear, "Bye, asshole."

He stepped over the dead body and went into see his mother. She was conscious and bleeding from a gash in her head, but her injury was not as bad as Cam had expected.

He sat her up against the bed, got a towel for her head and said, "Mom, just sit there for a minute and I'll take you to the hospital." She was still stunned so she just did what Cam said, not knowing what had happened out in the hallway.

Cam stepped out the front door and as a cool fall breeze hit his face and seemed to slow time. He wondered if this was a sign of freedom from living with an abuser or his last breath of freedom.

He told his sister to go down to Jimmy's house and get him. "Tell him to come quick. There's an emergency."

As Cam was talking with his mother in the bedroom to reassure her that she was going to be alright, Jimmy entered the house. Cam walked down the hall, grabbed his sister by the shoulders and hugged her into his chest.

After a few seconds, he turned her around and told her, "Wait outside."

He quickly explained to Jimmy what had happened and told him, "I palmed the screw driver into his heart and I think that's going to get me into big trouble."

Jimmy spent a few seconds looking around and said, "No you didn't." "He fell on his face and the floor caused it to go in farther. Now help me get him over on his face."

After they rearranged the body Jimmy stepped in front of Cam while he looked into his eyes and said, "You look too clean to generate much sympathy. Plant your feet and close your eyes."

Cam took a deep breath because he knew what was coming and as soon as his eyes were shut Jimmy hit him square on the nose sending blood everywhere. Karate had already made sure Cam's nose wasn't a virgin.

As Cam opened his eyes Jimmy said, "That bat needs a little of your blood on it. I'll take your sister home with me. She and I were never here."

After letting the nose blood soak his sweatshirt, Cam got another towel for his nose and drove his mom to the hospital. The ER admitting nurse called law enforcement and Cam explained how he was attacked and hit with the bat. He told the cops that he used the screw driver that was handy to stop the beating. After a brief investigation, the case was closed as self-defense. Apparently, the dead stepdad had prior arrests for domestic abuse that confirmed Cam and his mom's statements.

Looking back as an adult Cam felt no guilt or remorse for his actions that day. He was a true Darwinist and believed that what happened that day was exactly what should have happened. He believed in society's rules and laws, but only as long as they resulted in justice. He wasn't about to set himself or anybody else up for an unjust outcome if he could help it. What he did come away with was a confirmed belief that you had to make situations work in your favor and not let circumstances dictate outcomes. It wasn't that he disregarded the law or truth. He had the upmost respect for both, but sometimes in life situations occurred that required an individual to deal with threatening events as best he could and often without a good option. He never told anybody the true story about what he and Jimmy did that afternoon because a secret isn't a secret if you share it. Some things are best confessed after you die. He viewed the compelling need of many people to confess as childish weakness.

The real irony always rolling around Cam's mind was that Jimmy later became a criminal defense attorney. Cam wondered if he was still staging crime scenes with his frighteningly quick imagination. He had to be humble under the circumstances but he did think most defense attorneys should place a – before the phrase defense, not after, on their business cards where it said: "Criminal Defense Attorney."

SIAMESE IN BLUE

The next two months in patrol division proved to be long for Cam and Bobby while they waited to hear about the gang assignment. Nothing ever moved fast within the police department administration. Every decision had to be analyzed, vetted, reanalyzed and committeed before it trickled up the chain of command and then back down. Some patrol officers thought it was management's deliberate attempt to torture underlings. Every day they dressed up in the blue suit with body armor, gun belt and all the other equipment, they wondered if they would ever be able to get out of uniform and do police work in street clothes. This was the irony of a police career. Cops, when they're rookies, can't wait to get into uniform. A few years later they can't wait to get out of it. The worst thing you can do to undercover cops is transfer them back to patrol where they have to don the blue suit.

As Cam and Bobby were about through with a shift one evening, they got a domestic violence call. What they really wanted was for dispatch to give this to a car that was just starting its shift so they could check out and go home, but that wasn't going to happen tonight because they were too backed up on calls for service. Cops hate DV calls because the combatants can't agree on anything but their mutual contempt for law enforcement. Often the call originates from neighbors who have had enough of the yelling and swearing. The fighting couple didn't request your service and doesn't want you there. The times when the wife does call for the police its often because she's scared, but that doesn't mean she'll cooperate. "Just tell him to leave," is not something cops are allowed to do. To top off the problem of uncooperative combatants, cops had to stay sharp because of the potential for danger. You were on someone else's home turf where weapons could be a real problem, since most people are saturated with guns and kitchens are full of sharp instruments, not to mention children, biting dogs, and alcohol and drugs being thrown into the mix.

Prior to going into the house Bobby said, "Stand by one Cam, I want to run these people and see what we're getting into." Cam, as usual, watched in amazement as Bobby ran car plates, addresses, and names through several databases to learn about the people who lived at this address.

After a couple of searches Bobby, said, "Okay, nothing scary, let's go." Cam always waited quietly because he knew how valuable information was to survival.

Since Cam didn't possess the required patience with these types of calls for personal reasons Bobby didn't fully understand, the general agreement was that Bobby took the lead. As they weaved their way through broken tricycles and trash to get to the run-down house with too much crap piled on the floor and two screaming spouses, Bobby stopped and rested up against an open dirty door casing for a minute. With his arms folded across his chest he just watched as the two combatants hurled accusations at one another as he stood in the open doorway.

"You're just a demanding bitch."

"Well you're such a fool that the cops have to come to your home."

And on they went. Hands were flying and spit was spraying as they vented every angry thought they ever had about one another. Bobby wasn't about to get a word in or get them calmed down as long as they were in this state of mind, so he did the next best thing. He walked over to the broken down brown couch that looked like a land fill reject and sat down. He found the remote control and turned up the TV. After channel surfing for a while he found a home renovation program he liked, put his feet up on the coffee table, took a handful of popcorn that was in a bowl on the couch and relaxed. Cam assumed Bobby's old door jam and watched in amusement with a smirk on his face.

After a minute or two the couple were so perplexed by Bobby's behavior that they stopped screaming and the husband asked, "What the hell do you think you're doing?"

Bobby said, "Well I'm here to talk about your loud fighting that's disturbing your neighbors, but that can wait cause I really like this show and it never works to make people stop till they're ready." He turned up the volume, munched a few kernels and started to watch the program again.

The couple couldn't stand it. They both just stared at Bobby. Then the husband said, "OK, we're ready to talk."

Bobby, still watching TV, said, "You sure, cause I don't mind. I like this show."

They both said, "Yes....yes" and stepped in front of the TV.

Bobby said, "Well Okay," as he turned the TV off and stood up he said "Well, why don't you tell me who you are and what caused all this ruckus tonight." As they identified themselves Bobby shook hands, then introduced himself and Cam, who just nodded at the two. After about 15 minutes of low key conversation Bobby had convinced the two marital enemies that screaming was not going to solve much and that sometimes it was best to not try to control your spouse but to accept them the way they were, warts and all.

They agreed with Bobby and promised not to fight anymore, at least tonight. They actually thanked Bobby for coming to their house and talking with them.

"We really appreciate you coming over tonight Officer Wright. You're really a good guy."

As Bobby and Cam crawled back into their unit to handle the next call Cam told Bobby with a smile on his face "Working with you is like having Dr.Phil for God damn partner."

Bobby said, "Maybe Dr. Phil should work on your foul temper and bad language."

Cam said, "Bobby, don't start on me about my swearing with that Moonie bullshit philosophy of yours or I'll hurt your feelings with logic."

Bobby said, "I doubt it."

"Okay Bobby, for instance, how did Adam and Eve populate the world without incest? I studied a little biology in college and if they were the only two people on earth they must have been keeping it in the family or else they were nailing the monkeys. That would explain you Jesus freaks."

Bobby said, "No doubt about it. You're going to hell." He started to laugh and said what he always said when he wanted to see Cam lock up his jaws in anger. "Cam, don't worry about that hell thing, I'll pray for you." Then as Cam's grip doubled on the steering wheel, Bobby laughed some more and thought, "Two family beefs quieted in under 30 minutes."

∞

As Cam and Bobby started their shift the next day Cam's mind was spinning. He was not predisposed to letting things move at their own speed. He truly believed in moving things along if he could.

He and Bobby were driving around their beat killing time after a lull in calls, when Cam said, "Bobby, how could we encourage administration to pick us for the gang unit?"

"Well, busting some gang members for something serious would be a good start and it wouldn't hurt if it was one of those self-initiated things that shows we're self-starters."

Cam thought about it a while and said, "Ya, that's a given, but the question is how do we do that. We know who some of the players are if we could just catch them holding some dope or doing a rip off." They drove around for a few more hours, handled a few calls and came up with at least a half dozen lame ideas that they immediately discarded. Frustrated, they fell into a silent patrol mode where they drove around, the Story Road and King neighborhood both racking their brains with little results. They were up to their eyeballs in drug addicts and gangbangers and they were still drawing a blank.

Dispatch broke up their dead-end thought process and assigned them to back up another unit that was dealing with a fight at an amusement park. This kiddy park had go-cart rides, video arcades, and a lot of roller coaster rides. A group of six gang bangers, who were 14 or 15 years old, had soaked a rival gang member's girlfriend on a boat ride. Each boat was equipped with a couple of water spraying guns and cannons. It was a given that everybody on this ride would get wet, but the boys overdid it on this girl. They had decided that if they really soaked the braless girl with the thin cotton top they could get an x-ray look at her boobs. Three different boats all circled to spray their target, which was the hot girl all dressed in white. The very wet boyfriend sitting beside her figured out the conspiracy and after they disembarked, was trying to fight all six of the younger punks for the honor of his angry lady with the cold, wet nipples.

The assigned officer was corralling the boyfriend while Cam and Bobby were IDing the young crew. When they had them all quieted down Cam went over to the older boyfriend who was an obvious tattooed gang member and removed his cell phone from his pocket.

The boyfriend started to protest, but Cam said, "Someone at the park called into the station to make a false report and I have to check it out." After a few minutes, he walked over to the other six punks and took their phones one at a time to examine them also. While this tactic wasn't exactly legal, it wasn't really a problem unless you found evidence of a crime that you were trying to get admitted into court.

The assigned officer, Don, kicked all of the punks out of the park and told them, "If I have to deal with you guys again today you're all going to jail after I Taser your dumb asses."

Don Clout was old school and was hoping he could survive all this "politically correct community policing shit" before he retired. When he signed on to the police department the only requirement was that you had to be big, tough and you were not required to be overly polite. He only had a few months to go, then it was off to Coeur d'Alene Idaho, a place cops called Blue Heaven because so many law enforcement officers retired there. Lowlife life-styles turned even the most tolerant cops into closet bigots. It wasn't a race thing. It was more about bad behavior that slopped over into other people's lives. Don wanted to go to a place that didn't have ghettos, low riders, gangs, rap music, sagging pants, tweakers, and a crime rate that was off the chart.

He walked up to Cam and said, "What's with the bullshit about a false report, Cam? We didn't get anything from dispatch."

Cam said, "I just wanted to see who the little shits were talking to."

Don grumbled with a serious snarl on his face and said, "Just don't be causing me any trouble. My god damn feet are killing me and I only got 5 months, 7 days, and 4 hours to go. Those political whores downtown would just love to steal my pension." He walked off toward his patrol car grumbling without waiting for a response from Cam. The sound of bad hip-hop music blared in the background over cheap park speakers, convincing Don once again that this contemporary culture was a sucking cesspool full of self-indulgent techno geeks that had no purpose in life and shit for taste when it came to music.

Bobby and Cam got back in their unit and went back in service.

Bobby looked at Cam and said, "He's a grumpy old fart."

Cam said, "Ya, but he did give me some inspiration."

Bobby was about to ask what Cam was talking about when Cam said, "Do you remember a month ago when grumpy Don and the other old guy Ed who works in the evidence room were talking about the crap they use to pull back in the old days."

"Ya, I guess."

Cam smiled and explained, "They used to get a major crook on the phone and tell him the narcs were on their way to his house with a search warrant. When he had gathered up all his dope and was driving away they would find a reason to stop him and make a big bust, all based on pure bluff and bullshit."

"And your point?"

"I've just acquired a big batch of current cell phone numbers of some serious bangers. How's your Spanish? You did learn to speak the lingo when you were trying to brainwash poor hungry little Mexican children into your church, right?"

Bobby said, "Oh, I can get by. The problem is my accent sucks."

"That's okay, Bobby. We'll make it quick and garbled since it's over a cell and out of a car."

Bobby was a little worried about this caper. He told Cam, "Oh, I'm sure nothing could go wrong with this plan."

"Faith, Bobby. Faith."

Cam told Bobby, "Head back to the station so you can do that voodoo you do with all these cell numbers and names we gathered up from the punks." They could have done most of the research from the MDT, but in-car computers had their limits and they really needed to access police department records to crunch all the information they had gathered. Cam called dispatched and cleared a 10-19 for follow up. They ran all the names, got their birth dates and home addresses, and decided to exclude the juvenile suspects as targets for their scam. They figured it wasn't likely they'd be holding big amounts of dope. Though the young gang members did have some older more serious gang members in their contact lists and the older boyfriend had a few heavyweights on his. The cell phone companies provided the owner identification. Cam cross-referenced the adult names with arrest records and came up with two guys what had thick rap sheets with dope arrests on them. He held up the paperwork with his left hand and slapped it with the back of his right.

"Here are our targets Bobby. Which one looks good to you?"

"Both. Why do it half way."

Cam nodded his head, "You're one of those guys who would drink all the Cool-Aid, aren't you, Bud?"

Over the course of the next few days Bobby and Cam decided to learn as much about the two target gang members as possible. Cam talked with the narcs and gang squad to pick their brains about these two and also to make sure he wasn't going to burn something they had going on with these guys. The best way to get rejected from a special unit was to screw up one of their ongoing investigations. Bobby did more research on cars they drove, their jobs and other family members. He also ran them through WSIN (Western States Information Network) to see if any other jurisdiction besides theirs had any active investigation related to these guys.

Bobby told Cam, "I don't think there's a perfect time or day to hit these mopes. But since we're taking a shot in the dark I'm guessing the 2nd or 3rd day of the month might be best because they, all their buddies and family members just got their welfare checks. It's more likely our boys will be holding then."

Cam was nodded his agreement with Bobby's logic and told him, "Okay, we have next Thursday the 3rd as a target date. You know their activity patterns best. Who's first and where do we take them down."

Bobby said, "Got it all worked out, Cam-e-ron. You just talk with dispatch and make sure we have some slack from calls for an hour or two. Of course, we might not need it if these two guys have one brain cell between them and just ignore the phone call."

∞

Vladimir Gonzales was a 28-year-old excon whose mother had had a brief horizontal encounter with a Russian immigrant. She couldn't pronounce his last name but always thought the name Vladimir was classy, so she used it for a first name on the byproduct of their "glasnost." He was trying to be a good dad this time when he got out of prison and he wasn't hanging with the guys that much anymore. He did, however, have to spend a little time with the gang to keep his connections solid for his heroin distribution business. He was one of the poor victims, according to the media, of an overzealous law enforcement system that sent non-violent drug defendants to jail.

When he got the garbled phone message from Bobby it sounded like one of his connections from Oakland. All he really heard in that three-second phone call was that the guy was being booked and overheard the narcs say they were going to Vladimir's house with a search warrant. He wasn't taking any chances. I mean, how many Vladimirs could there be in San Jose?

He yelled at his old lady to "Get the kids in the truck-- Now!" and went out in the back yard where he had his dope stashed. He figured kids and his old lady would be good cover and make him look like a family man out running errands. The shovel was leaning against the rusted out old tool shed and three feet away from where Vladimir dug up a piece of turf that had a broken pot sitting over it. About a foot deep in the soft soil was a one-pound plastic bag inside a Tupperware bowl full of black tar heroin. As he got into the lowered Chevy pickup truck he stuffed it under the front seat and drove away with the whole family. He noticed that his little girl, who was two years old was in the center front seat in her booster car seat but his little boy who was seven wasn't belted in the back, half bench seat.

"Bitch, get the belt on the kid. I can't be gettin pulled over for shit like this!" Vladimir yelled. As his wife undid her seat belt to get the young boy buckled in, Bobby pulled the marked unit up behind them like a hawk in flight ready to hit a mouse.

They were still on a residential street driving less than 5 mile an hour but Vladimir knew he was screwed when his old lady said, "Shit, the cops."

He figured, correctly, that the cops had all the legal cause they needed to stop him since his old lady and kid didn't have a seat belt on, so he reached under the front seat and pulled out the zip lock bag of heroin. Hiding it was not going to be easy because the cops were watching him through the rear window of his truck, so wherever he chose had to be within reach. Then it hit him. The baby's diaper. No one would ever look there. Guys did everything in their power to avoid diapers and babies.

Cam smiled as he told Bobby, "He reached under the front seat. I saw his shoulder drop ever so slightly and then he handed something to the little woman."

"Ya, I saw it and she was messing with the kid in the car seat just after that. I'll bet if one of us were to pick up that baby to inspect the car seat we'd find something under that kid."

"Okay, Mr. Wright, light'em up." Bobby turned on the red lights and his rear flashers. The quiet residential street was void of people this time of day as most people were at work. Vladimir drove on for another half a block to give his woman time to stash the dope, so Bobby gave a short burst on the siren.

Cam said, "I'll be on the passenger window this time." This was not their typical traffic stop tactic. They liked to have the passenger officer hang back by the patrol car so that if shooting happened the officer up front could hit the ground and the rear officer could lay down cover fire into the car. Cam believed that tactic would risk the kids getting shot in this situation, so he chose to approach the passenger side.

"Watch both their hands good. He won't want to do his second strike. That's a long time in jail."

As they exited the unit Bobby said "10-4."

When Bobby approached the car, he was the picture of a low-key polite public servant making a routine traffic stop. Had the suspect and his woman turned to the passenger side of the car and seen Cam standing there with his hand on his gun and his thumb on the holster release they might have figured out that this was not quite a routine traffic stop. Bobby asked Vladimir for his driver's license, registration and proof of insurance, which required a bit of glove box diving, but the women eventually found all the paperwork. Bobby talked quietly about the importance of seat belts when driving, particularly with children. When he had all the paperwork he nodded to Cam and asked Vladimir to step out of the vehicle.

When he did, Bobby watched his hands and carefully and looked at his waist band for signs of a gun. Vladimir had been caught off guard when he left his house in such a hurry, so he was wearing a wife beater tank top tucked into his bagging jeans. This told Bobby that he probably didn't have a gun on him because it would be easy to see. Vladimir was suffering a little post-prison diet bulge so every fat fold and bulge showed under his too-tight tank top. As he was walking back to the rear of the car with the suspect Bobby pulled out his ticket book to start a citation. Vladimir was the picture of cooperation because he thought a seat belt ticket was a small price to pay for getting out of this mess without going to prison. Vladimir hoped these cops didn't understand gang tattoos because if they did they might spend some extra effort checking him out.

The tattoos showed his gang affiliation as well as the fact that he'd been an enforcer for the gang.

Cam tapped on the passenger window and asked the woman to get out of the car. Startled at the sound and sight of Cam outside her window, she stepped out, leaving the kids in their seats. He asked her if she had some identification so he could see in her purse. As she was opening her wallet he could see her purse wasn't holding anything lethal. She was dressed in a pair of jeans shorts and a loose tank top because of the hot weather and Cam noticed she didn't have shoes on because Vladimir rushed her out of the house. The Roman numeral XIV tattooed on her right breast made her gang background pretty clear.

After the citation was signed, Bobby asked Vladimir to step over to the curb with his partner for a moment.

He asked him "Do you mind if I look in your car and inspect the child safety seat?"

Vladimir didn't want to act suspicious so he said, "I guess it's okay."

Bobby knew that probable cause was one legal way to search a car, but consent would also work if he lost the probable cause in court. The probable cause was an inspection of the child safety seat and the seat belt. The hiding of something from under the front seat might make it through court but it was questionable because they really didn't have court admissible evidence of probable cause to believe it was dope. Now he had both legal search justifications consent and probable cause in case one fell apart in court. When both occupants were with Cam, Bobby opened the driver's door and leaned inside to look around. Both Vladimir and his woman were so nervous that Cam thought they might bolt so he asked them a few questions to distract them while Bobby did his thing. Bobby talked quietly to the baby and the other child while he released the carrier seat belt to get the kid out of the car seat. He'd done this a million times at home. When he put his right hand under the kid to remove him and his left under the kids arm pit he felt the large ziplock and could actually see part of it between the baby's jumper snaps. He pulled it out partway and could see it was a black tar ball the size of a baseball wrapped in transparent plastic wrap. Bobby decided he would leave the zip lock in place for photos. He left the baby in the car and stepped around the back with a smile on his face as he put his hand on his gun.

He said, "Mr. Gonzales you're under arrest." Cam grabbed the back of Vladimir's pants and T-shirt so that his feet were barely touching the ground as he pushed him over the back of the truck bed. Bobby had him cuffed before he knew what was happening.

As Bobby was searching and stuffing his prisoner into the back of his unit, Cam was cuffing the woman. She offered no resistance but was worried about the kids. Cam assured her they would call a relative to come get them. He performed a quick pat down of her pockets. Then Cam put the women in the rear seat with Vladimir. He sat down in the driver's seat of the patrol car for a minute and turned off the police radio and turned on a small tape recorder. He placed it on the center duty bag that carried all their equipment just so the mic was pointed at the back seat, then he joined Bobby in securing the evidence. They retrieved some of the paper-work and made some calls to get an ID officer and the kids picked up before they transported their prisoners. As they were driving to jail Cam rewound the tape and turned the volume up so that everyone could hear it.

The tape showed Vladimir was in a full-blown rage screaming at his woman, "You didn't hide the shit well enough and now I'm going back to the joint and it's all your fault you stupid bitch."

Bobby and Cam smiled at each other because all of it would be used in court because there is no legal expectation of privacy in the back of a patrol car, so recorded conversations were admissible evidence. The charge of possession of heroin for purposes of sale, based on the quantity of dope, had a hefty prison sentence for a repeat offender. To top it all off, Vladimir had used a minor to transport drugs, which was an additional heavy-duty charge that would net him some extra prison time.

After they booked their prisoners and were walking back to their patrol car Cam reached over and gave Bobby a big hug, lifting him off the ground, "Fucking magnificent Bobby!"

Bobby started laughing and said, "Ya, it was pretty great huh? We still have time left to hit #2. What do you think?"

"Why not. If you want to get noticed two is better than one."

∞

Oscar Gomez wasn't into heavy weight drugs like Vladimir. He was a weed dealer. They'd discussed maybe going for a crook that was dealing more serious drugs, but settled on Oscar. The thing that attracted Bobby and Cam to him was that he was heavily ganged up since he was 13 years old, which was 10 years ago, and he never stopped dealing weed no matter how often he got popped. Bobby laid in the call using a combination of English and Spanish slang to make his accent a little less noticeable.

As they waited with a view of the front of Oscar's house to see if the crook was going to drive away they had begun to think it wasn't working. Maybe Oscar was too smart to take the bait. Fifteen minutes later, just when Cam was thinking, one out of two ain't bad, the front door flew open and Oscar stuck his head outside. Looking both ways cautiously, he stepped out and walked to his car with a very large gym bag. He drove away fast and was going at least 20 miles per hour over the posted speed limit, so Cam had all the legal cause he needed to stop him. Cam ditched the carton of chocolate milk he was drinking as he activated the reds. Oscar floored his low rider Honda. They turned onto Willow Ave heading west which is a major crowded city traffic route and were going at least 60 mph, weaving around slower cars. Oscar started to throw kilo-sized bricks of weed out the driver's window as Bobby radioed in the chase.

Cam was laughing while he was driving, "Guess he doesn't want to be caught with weed in the car." Bobby started laughing too and after this rolling pot disposal car drove for about two miles dumping weed about every 500 yards, it pulled over.

A CSO (community service officer) for the department was tracing the disposal route and gathering up what pot she could find, although much of it was dispersed by cars driving over it. A few good citizens stopped and retrieved some evidence that they would eventually neglect to turn in.

As Cam and Bobby approached the car they started to laugh again because the whole interior of the car was covered in pot debris as was Oscar himself. The windows were down and it made the debris, float all over the car. He had it in his matted curly hair, beard, and ears. His clothes were covered with the stuff. Several bricks of weed were found on the floor of the car. They pulled him out of the car and waited for the CSO to come take pictures of him before they booked him and had the car seized for evidence. On the way to jail, whenever Cam looked at Oscar covered in pot in his rear-view mirror, he would break out in laughter.

Oscar just hung his Jerry Garcia looking weed cover head in shame and kept saying, "I'm so fucked. I am sooooo fucked."

∞

At 53 years of age, Sergeant Bud Glen was a legend at the agency. They gave him the gang detail because he was famous for carving things out of the wilderness. He had done it with the narcotics squad, the SWAT team, and now gangs. Whenever the brass needed a job done, Glen was their go-to guy. The only problem was he ruffled a lot of feathers. To say he wasn't politically correct was a bit mild. In fact, he was downright archaic.

When the chief was explaining the implementation of the newest affirmative action program to increase minorities, gays and diverse officers a few years back, Glen muttered loud enough for everyone to hear, "Swell, I'll be up to my belly button in runts and cunts." It was little comments like this that made administrators cringe and look around to see who from the outside might have heard it.

He was, however, exceptionally good at unconventional details like gang units because he was creative and aggressive. He allowed his people to be the same way, but if they got too far out of line his 6-foot 5-inch height and 250 lbs. was enough to scare them back in line. He was hired before affirmative action height and weight requirements changed when cops had to be big and tough. The standing joke was that he wasn't actually born, he was a collection of parts from someone's basement. There was a famous story that followed him around. Apparently, a street freak spit on him and flipped him off one day, mistaking age for infirmity. Glen grabbed the guy's bird finger and a hand full of genitals as he threw him completely over a parked car.

Sergeant Glen had a small tattoo on the inside of his left forearm that looked like a stick man. It had a circle with a line going down and a single line crossing it at a right angle. When a rookie cop told one of Glens older buddies that a stick man was a dumb tattoo, Glens buddy explained that it was common during the mercenary wars in Africa to get your blood type, like O+ tattooed on your arm because a correct transfusion might save your life. This tidbit of information only increased Glen's already considerable mystique.

Glen called Bobby and Cam into his office and told them that they (the two gang busting heroes) had gotten their requested transfer. He explained that they would be partners for at least six months and maybe longer since everybody else was already partnered up and they were the only transfers for a while. He told them that they would generally work in plain clothes but that occasionally they'd be in uniform for special details. The unit was unique in that they investigated a variety of crimes. The only requirement was that they usually have some link with gang activity, but since gangs were into everything it gave Glen a wide jurisdiction. On occasion they would be used for other police duties like riots, manhunts, stakeouts and anything else bizarre that came along.

Bobby and Cam were so jazzed about their new assignment they could barely contain themselves. Not only was it new and interesting but it came with a pay raise and an undercover car.

After they left the Sergeant's office Cam was ready to celebrate and asked Bobby, "You want to get in your van and come over to my house for a celebration beer?"

Bobby gave Cam a tired look and said, "I don't drive a van and I don't drink beer."

Cam smirking, said, "I know."

Bobby smiled back at Cam and said, "But if you think you're brave enough, tough guy, my wife and family are having a picnic at the park and I'm sure they won't mind if I bring a heathen."

Cam looked at Bobby like he was kidding but soon realized he was serious. "I don't know, Bobby, what if I slip and swear or something."

Bobby grinned, "Pretend you're visiting a grammar school on Officer DARE night." Cam stared at Bobby and gave him a dirty look.

Cam had to do a short stint at a grammar school as a School Resource Officer to finish a contract for another officer who got sick. One of the department comedians used to do an imitation of Cam as Officer DARE, "Just say no to fucking drugs you little shits." This got back to Cam, and Bobby loved to tease him with it.

So Bobby and Cam went to the park, ate hot dogs, drank lemonade and played a friendly game of softball with the Wright family. Cam did find a girl who captured his imagination. A cousin of Bobby's was as cute as they come with a body to match. The bright sun shining through the elm tree foliage made her look like she was out of some scene from a 1950's Bible movie. Cam was blown away by her big white caffeine free smile which reminded him of another girl whose company he really missed.

On the way back from the park Bobby noticing the mutual attraction between his cousin and Cam, said, "You know that she's not like a lot of the girls you date, Cam?"

"Don't sweat it Bobby. She's cute but I'm not getting married just to get laid and besides I might not be able to perform if I saw that funky underwear you dudes wear."

Bobby just shook his head and said, "I'm sorry sometimes I even talk to you."

What Cam wouldn't tell Bobby was that he had fun and after meeting his family he now understood why Bobby had such an upbeat view of the world. To tell Bobby that would just ruin his perfectly honed reputation.

Cam also wondered why he hadn't called the woman he missed so much, who kept invading his dreams. But that's something he was truly afraid to address. It would require that he be a mature adult and he wasn't sure he was ready for that.

∞

Cam found the gang detail to be everything he'd hoped for: lots of freedom to make good cases and tactically smart guys to work with. The Sergeant was cool too. He told you clearly what he wanted and didn't over supervise you.

Bobby liked it also. He enjoyed booking thugs and cleaning up neighborhoods even if it was just temporary. The sense of freedom was like taking a tropical vacation. They got to dress in blue jeans and T-shirts, drive an undercover car and their hours were flexible unless they had a combined operation where the sergeant needed a bunch of bodies. A lot of what they did was narcotics related and often they teamed up with the drug taskforce because gangs get most of their money by dealing drugs. Cam was learning a lot and getting good at drafting search warrants. He had writing them down to where he could get one in a couple of hours. The new computer software helped because once you had your expertise paragraph written, the suspects and the house described, it was just a matter of putting in your specific investigation material. The rest was boiler plate language that the software template gave you. The result was that you caught a lot of crooks with guns and drugs.

Cam and Bobby were happiest when they were challenged and learning all the skills required to be an effective gang squad member was challenging. This assignment forced officers to think outside the box because you couldn't get anything done by being afraid to try new things.

One afternoon Bobby noticed a kid he had helped out a couple of years back walking home from school. Bobby had helped the kid get his bicycle back from some neighborhood punks that strong armed it from him. The Buena Vista area was famous for making life rough on kids. He and Cam had been doing some drive-by surveillance on a school that was having gang recruitment problems. Bobby was driving so he waited till Ray had walked several blocks away from the school and other kids before he pulled across the street to chat him up a little.

He talked the kid into meeting him at the library later that afternoon. He figured that a library would be safe because that's the last place you'd find a gang member. He and Cam bought a Coke for Ray, now a sixteen-year-old, and started to pump him for gang information. He was starting to dress like the local Mexican gang members and Bobby figured he was a wannabe. When they got enough information from him about who the bosses were and what they were up to, Bobby figured he had enough to do a search warrant.

He was surprised by how cooperative Ray was but attributed that to the fact that he'd helped him when he'd been ripped off. Cam was getting good at playing word games when he was drafting warrants, and even though it was a stretch to establish the probable cause the law required, it could work. The current case law standard allowed officers to use the "totality" of the information they received to justify a warrant and didn't hold them to the strict standards used in the past of the "Aquilar" case. They gathered information from a couple of different sources to make their legal justification for a search warrant. Ray's information was just a part of the case.

When they got the warrant drafted they gave it to the Sergeant for review. This warrant was for the search of a house on West 19th street and a crook named Alfredo. There was reportedly marijuana and meth being sold there.

He looked it over and smiled as he told Bobby, "You're full of crap, but I like your work ethic. See if you can get it signed. What's the worst thing that can happen? You get rejected by a judge. Now wouldn't that be a new damn experience?"

A very busy judge who happened to be tuning up his BMW motorcycle at the time didn't read the whole warrant because his hands were greasy and he was irritated that these two cops had come to his home and were interrupting his off-duty activities. He told Cam to turn the pages so he could read it as he was wiping his hands on a red mechanic's rag. He would nod his head every time he wanted Cam to turn the page and Cam knew that even a speed reading judge who was trained to plow through tons of paperwork every day couldn't read that fast.

The judge looked up from the paperwork and said, "Your pen!" Then Cam held the warrant opened to the signature page on top of the judge's motorcycle seat and he signed it. They were off.

Cam and Bobby told the Sergeant that they had a warrant ready to go but Sergeant Glen told them, "Chill boys," they'd brief at 6:00 a.m. sharp the next day. So, at 6:00 am they had rounded up another five squad members for the raid. The briefing was led by Bobby explaining the players and what they had in the house. They were looking for guns, stolen property and drugs but the main goal was to identify some out of town gang members who were guiding this pack of younger thugs. The shot callers were a little older and had served joint time so the concern was that these locals would soon become more violent and aggressive.

Patrol was called as a backup because of the bad neighborhood. When everyone was in position they hit the house. Sergeant Glen always kept an eye on fresh gang squad members when they were new at serving warrants because it was controlled chaos when armed officers kicked in a crook's front door.

They managed to catch everyone asleep because they hit it at 7:10 am. Day service of a warrant requires that it be after 7:00 a.m. and before 10:00 p.m. Outside of those hours you need a judge to endorse the warrant for night service and that was more difficult to get. You had to show why you needed to go into the house at night. Case law held that "a man's home is his castle" and extra justification for violating privacy during sleeping hours was required. Fortunately, daytime for normal people was still bed time for dirt bags. One half asleep parolee that had crashed on the couch staggered to the door and opened it when Bobby knocked. As he opened the door and saw a half dozen cops standing on the porch he realized too late that he was in trouble. Bobby gave the required announcement, "Police Officer – Search Warrant," before he pushed open the door and everyone fanned out to gather up the occupants. The unit identified a bunch of new players mixed in with the usual suspects and ran them all for warrants, probation conditions and parole status. Two probation officers who were working that day dropped by the house to deal with a couple of their clients. At least four gang members went to jail for felony violations and a few more for probation and parole holds. Seven guns were seized, about 2 oz. of meth and several pieces of stolen property. Three kids were placed with CPS (Child Protective Services), which added a few additional charges. All in all, it was a good warrant. When you made cases like this it set multiple agencies and legal processes in motion. It was like throwing a rock into a pond. Waves rippled out and took on a life of their own.

Bobby told Cam, "Serving a search warrant is a lot like being on a treasure hunt when I was a little kid. This is fun stuff when you get their goodies."

Cam just chuckled and nodded.

Cam had inserted language into the warrant that asked the court that they be authorized to search for records or documents showing sales of drugs. That language allowed officers to read any written material in the house. Random intelligence investigations would be outside the scope of the warrant because the 4th amendment requires that warrants must state specifically things to be searched and seized and what crimes they related to. Fishing expeditions aren't allowed. Fortunately, Cam was one step ahead. They gathered all types of paperwork that showed new crimes avenues that these thugs were expanding into.

As Bobby and Cam sat at their gray metal desks back at the unit headquarters they plowed through stacks of documents, some handwritten, some on computer drive, a few type printed. The gang unit had a reasonably modern office but the desks were generally set in rows next to one another and with their desk backs meeting the back of another row. Only the sergeant had his own office. Cam looked to his left to see Bobby and straight across from him was Erin. Several piles of cardboard boxes were sitting on the floor behind and between Bobby and Cam. Cam removed a folder from one of the boxes and started to investigate what exactly they had seized.

Cam said, "Look at this file labeled "P" on this disk. It gives the city and a monetary amount per week by each number. It looks like dope sales but there's another list that has to be dope because it gives weights in grams."

Bobby said, "Could be girls, there are some photos in another box here somewhere, that I thought were their old ladies because they were full of porn shots, but maybe they're not girlfriends. Maybe they're victims."

Cam looked at Bobby with a pensive gaze and said, "Perhaps 'P' stands for Puta (whore) or Pussy. Real creative these morons."

Bobby said, "Guess we need to look over some missing person photos as well as booking shots to see if we have any matches. If we can identify some of these women maybe we can figure out exactly what they're up to."

"Ya, I guess, but most of those appear to be crotch shots so I don't hold out much hope for a match.

Good police work often resulted from combing through gross information and examining it in context with what you already know about the suspects. Then the job was finding out what crime they were involved in and getting the evidence. It was often fruitless work but then every once in a while, it would pay off. As they were sorting through all this raw data to try and understand the gang's activities they were told that the Sergeant wanted to speak to them.

∞

Sergeant Glen did not take a management motivational course from the famous Tony Robbins. He was more the General George Patton type. When he called Cam and Bobby in for a chat, they thought it was for an atta-boy on the successful search warrant.

He started off with, "You guys nailed a few dirt bags yesterday and seized some dope."

Cam said, "Ya, it turned out okay."

But the Sergeant wasn't there to talk about what was good about the raid, he was there to dig a little deeper.

"If you can find that much dope and that many assholes in your area, then perhaps you haven't been aggressive enough in shaking the damn tree. I mean shit man, this is a shot in the dark warrant based on bullshit and we find this many bad guys. No telling what's out there if you start doing real police work. I need you two modern cops to get your asses out there and make some shit happen. Twist some informants, jack up a few people, stop some cars, do some probation searches. Hell, I don't care what you do, but this raid tells me that we got wall-to-wall gang-bangers out there and I want to see a lot more of them going to jail. Got it?"

Bobby and Cam had heard about this lecture so they both just followed procedure as recommended by previous recipients of Glen's lectures and said, "Yes sir." Glen turned his back to the two officers by swiveling his chair back toward his desk. The conversation was over.

When they walked out of the Sergeant's office Bobby was a little bummed by the ass chewing and said, "Wow, I wasn't expecting that."

Cam told him, "Cheer up, partner. Do you know that this means?"

Bobby just looked at him waiting. "The gloves are off. We get to rattle their cage and the Sergeant will clean up after us. It's like a gift from heaven."

When they got into their undercover unit, a ratted out old black Mustang, Bobby took out a notebook and started to write.

Cam said, "What ya writing, Bobby?"

Bobby never looked up and said, "I'm making a chart that has tactics we can use on these gangs and then we can put down subheadings of things we tried and how well they worked. It will help us analyze what tactics worked best."

Cam just shook his head and said, "That's my boy, I'll bet you made notes on the night of your honeymoon so you'd know what makes the little woman jump."

Bobby just ignored him and kept writing.

After a few minutes Cam said, "Okay, Mr. Wright, what you got so far?"

"Well, just some of what the Sergeant said, probation search clauses, parole searches, twist informants and a couple I came up with were visit the jail at the start of every shift and see if there's anybody booked who would like to work off their beef snitching for us. We should also start meeting with the schools because some of my friends tell me that the older gang members are sending younger guys to recruit little girls even in the junior high schools."

Cam was quiet for a moment and told Bobby, "I apologize for my smart mouth. Those are actually some pretty good ideas. Put down we should meet with the narcs once a week to see if any of our boys are overlapping with theirs. We also should start thinking about a gang injunction although that really should be done on a higher level than us. Oh, let's not forget to chase down those photos and other intel you got from the warrant."

Bobby said, "We got a plan."

Cam added, "And let's not forget; just generally fucking with those pieces of shit. Especially the head turd, J-Tra."

Barrio University School of Business

J-Tra, AKA Juan Angel Travaldos was going to be a successful businessman no matter what. Working in the fields like his family did was crap and he'd rather be dead or in prison. At 27 years old, he was the youngest hombre in the city. There were older Nuestra Familia shot callers, usually fresh out of prison, that could tell him what to do but he was the man when it came to his boys. The members of his gang were Nortenos and there wasn't really any serious competition from other gangs in the immediate area. There was an occasional turf war with the blacks and Asians but the other Mexican gangs just didn't have the numbers to be a real threat. That didn't mean he wasn't required to do a few drive-bys or fuck up a few people now and then, but generally speaking, he owned his piece of turf.

Most of his crew were guys from the neighborhood that he knew and they brought in some of their friends, younger brothers and cousins, so control was easy. Besides, he was the only one who served real joint time, a three year stretch for auto theft, so he had instant respect. The problem was that the big boys who let him run his operation were constantly adding more members to their gang as they made parole, and they needed more of the cut to keep everyone happy.

When J-Tra showed them his version of the books (a school spiral notebook with approximations of earnings) they just kept saying, "You ain't doing shit. You should make more scratch than this." This was why he was expanding his operation into the ladies. They could make you almost as much as dope thanks to internet massage / porn sites, and you took a lot less heat for it. The problem was, it was a lot of work to recruit a good whore and it took a few months to get her programmed. It required a strong leader to get his crew working. Many of them were lazy and just wanted to get stoned, but he could get it done. He had to get it done. The only other option was to go back to where he used to live and that was not going to happen.

His mother and father were field workers from Michoacán Mexico and they dragged the kids along with them following the crop harvest, because they didn't have any place to leave them. When the kids were old enough they picked, too. His dad had a semi-retarded sister that would go to the fields with them and take care of the little kids, but when they were old enough to be out of diapers the young kids could pick and put it in their parents' bucket. They went to work so young that J-Tra couldn't remember not working. His dad got deported one night when he was out drinking up the day's wages with some friends. There was a bar fight and the cops just bagged all the illegals in the bar and gave them to ICE (Immigration and Customs Enforcement). J-Tra figured out later in life that his dad just seized opportunity and didn't come back to a miserable life that had too many mouths to feed and so little future. He often wondered if his cowardly old man was still alive and what he was doing. He'd like to meet up with him so he could tell him what a chicken shit thing he did to the family when he abandoned them. He often thought it might feel good to stick him good with the belt buckle knife he always wore.

That's why J-Tra had to make this way of life work, because he wasn't going to live like his parents did. Dope, whores, and gangs were his ticket out. He was smarter than your average gang leader. He read everything he could about gangs and crime tactics. He figured if he was smart he could increase profits and avoid getting busted again. He'd learned that you didn't want to handle dope or stolen property yourself, unless it was unavoidable, and that mules were expendable, just like any business overhead. He made it a point to listen to other old timers in the gang to get tips on staying out of jail. What he was hearing lately was what a sweet deal running women was.

Finding whores wasn't that tough if you weren't looking for fresh young stuff. The streets were full of strung out addicts and old hookers that could be recruited. They weren't dependable, but they could be intimidated or bought with their dope of choice. All he had to do was park a couple of thugs near a working girl and chase off johns or threaten the girls till they played ball. Once in a while you had to bitch slap them around to make them pay attention. J-Tra could even get them more tricks and free motel rooms if they played along. Protection was what it was all about. They worked with you and nobody messed with them.

Dory was a good example. She was pushing 35 but still looked good for a whore that had been using heroin for 20 years. She had been easy to recruit because she didn't have a good connection when her old man up and dumped her in San Jose. J-Tra and the boys became her source and she became one of their party girls. When she wasn't working the streets, she serviced the gang. One of the shot callers from the Nuestra Familia had taken a liking to her because he liked white chicks that were a little older. She was loaned out to him whenever he wanted, but J-Tra had to let her heal up for a few days afterwards before he could pimp her out again on the street. Manny Salinas was a little rough on his women.

It was the recruiting of young girls that was work. You had to find young dumb bitches that would fall in love with a gang member. The guy had to be a little older, good looking and dress a little better. He would treat the girl like a girlfriend and buy her things. Take her on dates and, most of all, get her stoned. Once he had her going down that road he could get her using more and more dope at parties and make sure she was leaving her old friends and family behind. Often this wasn't a problem because, like most predatory animals, the gang recruiters had a sixth sense for troubled girls from dysfunctional families who wanted to escape. She would become one of the 50,000 women trafficked in the U.S. every year.

After a few heavily intoxicated weeks it was just a matter of sharing the girl with his friends and taking lots of pictures for blackmail. He would tell her the next day that it was no big deal; it was a normal gang membership initiation ritual. Then a little more "sweet boyfriend" behavior mixed in with a dash of violence, then a little more sharing for money and an off-balance lost girl who liked her dope and was a afraid of her family seeing her porn pictures would just give in. A whore was born.

Some of the hard-headed bitches had to be force-fed dope. Or, if you were in a big hurry, you could do it that way. All you had to do was lock them down and get them strung out on heroin. They eventually would crave it so much that you could control them. You had to guard them while they were turning tricks at first but eventually you and the dope could control them.

It was a classic domestic violence model on how to keep a woman off balance and isolated, but pimps didn't read it in a textbook, they just felt it. This all took time, but if you could get a few years out of a whore before she ODed or ran off, you could make serious money pedaling her. If you worked a good looking young one and marketed her on the right websites you could net several grand a week. You could pay off the motel owners and clerks with blow jobs from the women. Whores were always good money but the business went exponential with the internet. Now girls could be sold to not just street guys but every horny fool with a computer. The beauty of it was if they got busted everything was in the girl's name and it was usually just a misdemeanor bust. And if she got too hot with the cops you could just trade some other out of town gang member for his girl.

It was easy and it wasn't as if the bitches mattered. They were just women, and that's what they were there for, to be used. At first, he'd felt bad when he raped one of them, or had to beat them around a little, but after a while it got easier. When he was in the joint doing his stay for auto theft, he got turned out. That's just the way the world is. Everybody takes what he can when he's on top and you got to get yours before someone else gets it and if that means some punk gets shot or some bitch gets hurt, tough shit.

J-Tra went to the gang house on 14th St. early that evening. The drinking had already started, so he had to get business done before everybody was too fucked up to listen. He told two of the younger good-looking guys, he liked to call his "pretty boys," that they had a quota to fill. He wanted a girl from each one of them ready and working in two months' time because he was getting heat from the Nuestra Familia bosses to get more money coming in. Manny Salinas was making veiled threats about replacing him if the splits didn't get better.

He told them to start working the junior high schools because johns like the young pussy and that these girls were dumber than regular high school girls. A few of the older guys were told to start working the street bitches and see if they could be recruited. Like any good boss, J-Tra set a deadline for production with a veiled threat of problems for non-producers.

After he handed out his marching orders for his troops he went to his mother's house because she liked to see him on Sundays for dinner. He thought briefly about how he treated his whores, and how he treated his female family members, but decided that it was different because his family mattered and the other women didn't. It was about respect and if someone tried to turn one of his sisters or cousins into a whore that would be disrespecting him and he'd have to kill them. That's just the way the world was. Protect your people and fuck the others. It's about the money and it's about respect.

J-Tra made sure he was wearing his neck chain with a crucifix to dinner because that was important to his mom. She gave it to him when he was 12.

THE OTHER ENEMY

Popular culture enjoys bad-mouthing defense attorneys, unless, of course, people are in trouble with the law, in which case they become your best friend. Cops are no exception and are, in fact, worse than the general population because they've usually been raked over the coals on the witness stand. But, every once in a while a cop will make a mistake. They'll drive drunk or have a fight with their spouse. Maybe a neighborhood dispute gets out of hand, or occasionally their kid pulls a major screw up. Then, even defense attorney-hating cops like defense attorneys.

Cam's childhood buddy had such a tough assed reputation as a criminal defense attorney that cops hired him to sue folks on occasion. The quote that often went with hiring him was, "I'm going to Jimmy Scallon your dumb ass."

Sergeant Glen said that "Hiring Jimmy Scallon was like putting a steroid fed herpes bug up someone's butt."

Jimmy liked his reputation and found that it not only generated business but also it made people fear him, and fear was power. He would often shut down potential legal problems with a tersely worded letter on his firm's letterhead. People just didn't want the acrimony or grief that came with the fight. Jimmy had a small law office with three other attorneys. They each had their specialty that made sure any potential client with money had an expert to represent them. Jimmy's was criminal law. He found that practicing law was not only fun but lucrative. He was in a word "doing well." He always made sure he dressed in the most expensive suits and ties he could find, and he always drove a car to match. It was part of his image. People didn't want to pay big money to someone who looked like a loser.

Every once in a while, Cam would go up against Jimmy on a bust he'd made. Jimmy loved to defend dope dealers because they had so much cash. Cam and the other cops, especially the narcs, would try to get asset forfeiture to seize all the money before the bust, but if they didn't find it all or didn't have time to seize it Jimmy could make serious money from a crook who was in no position to shop around for a cheaper deal. Besides, money was easy to come by if you were a dealer.

On one fairly big dope dealer case a couple of months ago, Jimmy got a big retainer and was fighting hard for his client. The problem he was having on this case was that the evidence against his client was overwhelming. That wasn't an impossible obstacle for a good attorney, however. Lawyers believe in the rule, "If you can't attack the evidence, attack the guy who brought the evidence." They were a lot like politicians, "If you don't like the investigation results attack the investigation." But then, come to think of it, a bunch of politicians are lawyers.

It was a standard tactic to attack on three fronts if you were a serious defense attorney. You filed a personnel complaint against the officer for misconduct. You filed a law suit against his agency for millions, and you plead your client not guilty and filed every obstruction motion you could think of. The government would often settle the case just to save money and make the headache go away.

As Cam took the stand to testify about his role in helping the narcs serve a search warrant on a crook, Jimmy started to cross examine him on his testimony. He used every defense attorney trick in the book to make Cam look bad in the eyes of the jury and then he asked the famous old defense attorney question, "Isn't it true, officer, that you wanted to arrest my client so bad that you rushed in that front door without waiting for him to respond to your knock and notice, thereby violating his 4th amendment constitutional rights?"

As Jimmy was pacing back in forth in front of the witness box, he turned his back to the jury and winked at Cam. Cam tried not to smile or to tell Jimmy out loud that he was a real prick. Eventually, after a weeklong, gut wrenching trial, the crook got convicted, Cam made his bust, and Jimmy got paid. He eventually got more money for the pending appeal, even though it was a million to one shot.

Defense attorneys always win because, like J-Tra, it's not about what's right or wrong, it's all about the money. Most claims about preserving the constitutional integrity of the court system were usually self-serving crap. Take away the money and most lawyers couldn't care less.

∞

Jimmy didn't used to be such a mercenary. Like a lot of new lawyers, he started out his law career with the best of intentions. He was going to help the down trodden and underprivileged. But after a few years of subsistence poverty, and repeatedly watching the justice system deviating from its purported goals, he'd become a bit jaded. Then there was the fact that almost all the people that got busted were dirty and deserved to go to jail. The final straw was when his dad, the owner of a small agricultural seed supply business, got screwed by the big boys.

Jimmy's dad had decided to buy a few acres for his business and stop renting. The piece of land and the warehouse were in a prime location and they were priced right so he bought them, only to find out six months later that the land was polluted by the previous owner with petroleum fuel. The EPA mandated cleanup would cost him huge amounts of money and the people he bought it from were no longer around. They had dissolved their business and the funds were gone. Jimmy was furious and, try as he may, couldn't get to the crooks that screwed his dad.

He made sure, that from that point on, to give special attention to big businesses that stepped on little people. They had not only stolen his father's money, but had destroyed his spirit. His sense of failure and humiliation were so destructive he never recovered and died a broken man. Many people focus on the monetary loss when someone gets scammed, but the real damage is usually to the victim's self-image. They often feel like a loser and a fool because they allowed someone to steal all their hard-earned money. Sometimes they even fail to report the scam out of embarrassment.

Jimmy's firm hired a ruthless partner to lodge civil suits against predators like the folks who stole his dad's money. Ambrose McCracken was let go from his previous firm because he was considered too much of a hard ass who wouldn't compromise and wasn't happy till he nailed his opposition to the wall. He was big, loud and aggressive with a shock of unruly white hair and eyebrows that seemed to be living entities. His personality was just fine with Jimmy. He could and did use a guy like this. Both Jimmy and McCracken handled the criminal cases, but when a good law suit came into view or a case with political overtones it was Ambrose who took over. He knew all there was about the lawsuit business.

He liked to say, "Anybody can sue anybody for anything. I can sue you for sodomizing your parrot but it won't fly in court. I mean the lawsuit, not the parrot," whereupon he'd burst forth with a belly laugh that would stop traffic. Ambrose knew that law suits are so expensive for big organizations like government agencies or corporations that they'll often settle the case just to avoid lengthy trials and expensive fees. It wasn't exactly extortion or a protection racket but then again it wasn't that far off. Ambrose knew every trick in the book and Jimmy often assigned him to cases where political strings had to be pulled because he had no shame and wasn't bashful about flexing the firm's muscle.

GRAB A PIECE OF ASS CURB HOLE

One of Cam's and Bobby's favorite past times while they were staking out crooks or otherwise killing time was to tell stories about the crazy nuts they worked with. So, as they were driving the Mustang past gang hangouts and problem schools they started to exchange stories.

Cam started by describing a cop by the name of Randolph Keen, a 35-year-old border-line geek who was the spitting image of the late Buddy Holly, including the glasses and greased down hair, who was always trying to sound tough by quoting and frequently misquoting TV or movie cops. Keen had pulled next to a car load full of petty crooks downtown one night in his patrol car and after he rolled down his window yelled at them, "grab a piece of ass, curb hole." This misquote would follow him for the rest of his career. Every time some other cop needed him to move out of the way they would tell him to "grab a piece of ass," or "don't be such a curb hole." As it was, the crooks that memorable day had no idea what he wanted them to do so they just drove on, till he lit them up with lights and siren.

Bobby's turn led to the story about the detective who, while staking out a dope dealer from an abandoned warehouse, found a dead petrified mouse and put it in his coat pocket. For the next three days he kept saying to the other officers "we need to do" this or that till someone inevitably said, "what's this 'we' shit, do you have a mouse in your pocket?"

Where upon he said, "Why, yes I do" and produced the mouse.

Cam told Bobby about a dispatcher named David who was continually finding that someone ate the tuna sandwiches he'd put in the squad room refrigerator. Everyone suspected it was a fat cop by the name of Howard, but there wasn't any proof.

One day, David sat down at the briefing table with all the officers who were about to go on shift and announced, "For the last two weeks someone had been stealing and, I assume eating, my sandwiches out of the squad room fridge. I just want the thief to know I've been making them out of cat food and I may have been adding a few disgusting things which I won't describe. Don't even ask what the mayonnaise really was!"

Howard turned three shades of blue, hurried from the squad room, and didn't talk on the radio for the entire shift.

Bobby reminded Cam about the time he dressed up a defensive tactics dummy in an interrogation room with a sweat shirt, sunglasses and watch cap. When a Sergeant with two days to go before retirement was walking by he beat the crap out of it with a night stick. The paranoid Sergeant was sure this incident was the one that would cost him his pension so he did his best Sergeant Schultz as he just kept walking and pretended he didn't see a thing.

Bobby was almost in tears laughing and asked Cam, "What kind of a sick mind would mess with an old Sergeant that way?"

Cam laughing told him, "The guy was a pain in the butt anyway."

With all this irreverent behavior fresh on his mind, Cam came up with an inspiration that would have serious ramifications much later.

They were driving by a junior high school that had been targeted by J-Tra's boys for recruitment. The gang members would show their colors while talking up the boys and girls. They often had some younger brothers and cousins that attended school there, so that was the excuse that allowed them on campus at the end of the school day. The principal had talked with gang unit officers earlier in the month about get extra patrol because she hated the fact that these young kids were being groomed to join the gangs.

Cam saw one older punk wearing his colors with his pants sagging under the cheeks of his ass. He was acting like a tough guy and hitting on the eighth-grade girls. Cam told Bobby to drive the car across the street and let him out.

Bobby, fearing the worse, said, "What's your plan, partner? You're not going to stir up a mess for us, are you?"

Cam said, "No, I'm just doing a little recon." As Cam got out of the car he quietly walked up behind the gang banger. Most people didn't pay any attention to Cam since there were a few other adults around picking up their kids and he was in plain clothes, which today meant blue jeans and Hawaiian shirt.

When Cam got right behind the punk he could hear him telling the kids about how cool his homies were and that "nobody fucked with them." His arms were flapping and fingers were pointing in typical barrio style like he was rapping his story.

Cam bent down grabbed the guy's pants and jerked them down around his ankles. The fool spun around to see who was trashing him and fell over, tripped by his own pants. As he was turtling around on his back trying to pull his pants up everyone was laughing at him. He eventually hauled his pants back up, got up and was trying to figure out what to do about this unbelievable insult. It was apparent he was unsure and a little afraid to start a fight with Cam.

Cam told him, "Hey, Hero, I hear you're a tough guy and your gang is respected. Do they all lay around on their backs with their pants down? You don't look so tough to me. You look like a big dip-shit."

The punk saw Bobby waiting next to the curb and figured them to be cops so he thought it over and walked away, threatening some terrible act of revenge in the future.

Bobby was glad the punk didn't take a swing at Cam because sometimes the result of a suspect trying to fight with him was unpleasant to watch.

When Cam and Bobby first started on patrol together they had made a stop on a car full of drunken street thugs. As they were starting to ID them, one of the punks swung on Cam. Cam deflected the blow with a quick left forearm and when the guy's arm was still in the air he karate punched him in the arm pit with a right half closed fist. Cam struck a nerve pressure point that made the guy fall to the ground and just twitch. As two other punks went for him, he kicked one of them in the chest, knocking him back into a car, and punched the other one breaking his nose. Bobby was relegated to cuffing the crumpled bodies.

This time, the punk that lost his pants made a good decision, even if he didn't know why. Bobby thinking that a little ass covering was in order stopped him, pulled out his portable radio and ran him through records to see if he had any wants or warrants.

He told Cam, "You must have thought you saw what could have been a gun, right?"

"10-4 Bobby, a pee shooter."

This sunny afternoon Mr. Punk wouldn't be recruiting for the gang at that school. Even the janitor and principal were laughing at this fool.

∞

Sergeant Glen told some of the unit members to show up in uniform the next day. Those officers who didn't have court would be assisting in a security detail at an auction site that did sales of asset forfeiture property for law enforcement. One of the add-on duties for a special squad was that you got snagged when they needed manpower for special incidents.

The detail started at noon so Cam and Bobby set aside the morning to go through the intelligence material they'd gathered at the search warrant with hopes of identifying some of the girls who were photographed.

If you got a picture of the face, you could try to match it with any number of data banks. The department did have a scanner but the photos had to be good and the scanner only matched ones that were close. It couldn't make an exact match for you. One of the best tools was to take a picture from the search and compare it to girls in the local high school's yearbooks. Every year the department got a free one from each high school to use for photo line ups. It was boring, time-consuming work but it paid off every once in a while.

After they worked at it all morning they had two possible identifications. Judy Beckett was booked for soliciting an undercover cop about a year prior and had a booking photo on file. They could get her information from the arrest report. The other girl looked like she might be a high school photo of Guadalupe Diaz. If it was Diaz, records showed she ran away at 17, which theoretically meant child sex abuse charges if you could get her to cooperate. The next step was to find them and see if they would talk. Not likely, but it had to be tried and eliminated as a possibility.

Unfortunately, all the investigative work on J-Tra's gang would have to wait. Sergeant Glen announced that Cam, Bobby, and two other sets of partners would be detailed to protect an auction for a six-hour shift. The owner of this property auction was a big political supporter of law enforcement and sold automobiles, boats, planes, jewelry, furniture and every other imaginable thing that law enforcement seized under asset forfeiture laws. Drug task forces were big suppliers of seized property for the auction. The owner also threw in other property he obtained by bulk purchases and inferred that it was seizure property thereby tricking the public into thinking it was a bargain. The money generated was staggering. All sales were done in cash, with no refunds, and the sale of one vehicle or boat could be tens of thousands. He hired off-duty bank tellers to handle the money and sent his wife around hourly to gather the cash and prepare the bank deposits to be shipped by armored car. The officers' role at this operation was to show up in uniform and stop any robbery, hopefully by a show of force.

As Cam arrived and met with the owner, he found that he was the senior officer present so he asked for a brief explanation of the operation. The owner just gave Cam a bare minimum explanation and told him where he wanted the officers deployed.

Cam listened and, after analyzing the situation, said, "Don't think that's going to work, Mr. Peterson. I'm not using my officers like a canary in a coal mine to detect a robbery. We will leave our marked units in front as a deterrent to let any potential robber know there are officers on site but my people are going to be in positions of cover and concealment so they have an advantage if a robbery occurs.

Mr. Peterson was unaccustomed to not having things go his way. He pointed his finger at Cam, "I pay your wages when you're on my auction site, you'll do as I tell you."

Cam smiled as he thought, "fucking with this arrogant asshole will be fun."

"No Mr. Peterson, you don't. The police department pays my wages and if you don't want us here, or don't like the service you're receiving, we can just gather our things and leave. You let me know."

Cam walked away and deployed his people the way he had felt best for their safety. Peterson was so angry that he instantly laid in a call to Sergeant Glen.

Glen listened for a few minutes then finally interrupted Peterson, "Mr. Peterson, my officer that I placed in charge will determine how his people will be deployed. That is none of your business. If you don't agree, feel free to not use our services in the future. Have a nice day."

Glen called Cam, "Cam, I just got a call from Mr. Peterson." Cam started to explain when Sergeant Glen interrupted, "Quiet and listen. Peterson's an arrogant prick who thinks people like us are expendable to protect his money. Do your thing out there, your way, but remember when you tell him to fuck off, don't use the word fuck. He'll be on the phone to the Chief first thing Monday morning. Got it?"

Cam smiled, "Yes sir."

He looked over at a smiling Bobby and said," When do we get relieved from this monkey fuck detail?"

Cam thought to himself, "Police work frequently required biting your tongue when amateurs tell you how to do your job." At least he had the Sergeant on his side.

That night as Cam and Bobby were securing all their equipment in the squad locker room Bobby said, "Cam, can you give me a lift to work tomorrow? My car is in the shop and my wife has a bunch of appointments and needs her wheels."

Cam said, "Sure, but I'm going to breakfast downtown at 7:00 a.m.

Bobby said, "Great, I'll be ready."

∞

Cam had to leave his place a little earlier than most officers because several years ago he found a rural piece of land with a tear down house on it. He told the realtor that the house would be perfect for his future mother in law. He really just wanted the land because he had put $500 down to hold a house that had to be moved off some development property. It wasn't that far away and had been his project place ever since. He and his five-year-old German Shepard Nick had a 3800-square foot half-done house to wander around in. The big place allowed Cam to pursue his oil painting hobby as well as fixing up an old Sunbeam sports car he liked to tinker with.

Bobby, on the other hand, lived in the suburbs where his kids had good schools and his wife was happy.

When Cam picked him up he had a passenger in the front seat. "Bobby, you remember Mr. White, don't you?

Bobby was surprised as he recognized the recent widower and said, "Ya, hello Mr. White."

Mr. White responded, "Call me Tom."

As they drove to the pancake house they talked about the latest San Francisco Giants game and the chances of the team making it to the playoffs. When they got to the breakfast diner, which was on their old beat, Cam slid into a booth next to a group of older retired guys that Bobby and Cam knew frequented this place for breakfast every morning. Cam said hello to the group since he'd had passing conversations with them before. As they started to order Cam picked up his portable radio and answered a call that Bobby thought was for someone else.

Cam said, "Crap, we got to take this call." Bobby and Cam got out of the booth and Mr. White stood up also prepared to go with them when Cam turned to the other old guys in the next booth and asked them if they could give Tom a ride home because he and Bobby had an emergency call to handle.

He said, "He's a military vet., like you guys, so I'm sure you boys can talk about making the world safe for democracy one woman at a time." Everyone laughed.

The guys said, "Sure" and told Tom to join then and order some breakfast. "We're just getting started." Tom had a genuine smile on his face for the first time in months. Cam patted him on the back and told him, "We'll do this later, okay?"

Tom, said, "Sure, no problem," and slid into the booth with his new friends.

As Bobby was following Cam outside he asked, "Did you really get a call or was that all staged."

Cam said, "You think I want to eat that greasy crap and shoot the bull with an old geezer all morning? Of course, it was a fake call."

Bobby just smiled, "I'll bet he becomes a regular now."

Cam said, "That's the plan. Now, all this warm and fuzzy shit has left a bad taste in my mouth. Whadaya say we go by the free clinic, get a bunch of condoms and leave them for the kids in the catechism classroom at the parish on 2nd street because if anybody needs protection...."

Bobby looked up and prayed that lightning bolts from above, thrown in anger, were smart weapons.

Hurry Up and Wait

Sergeant Glen sat in the Lieutenant's briefing room and listened to his meeting with the California Department of Justice. Glen really wasn't a participant since he was seated in one of the chairs lined up against the wall along with other Sergeants and detectives. He wasn't sitting with the elite at the table but the Lieutenant wanted him there so he wouldn't have to repeat things and so Bud could offer advice later. It was best to get Bud Glen's comments after the meeting and not in front of state officials. He could occasionally rub people the wrong way.

The whole purpose of this get-together was because DOJ wanted to borrow some manpower for a broad, multi-city stakeout. They had been having some armed robberies of card game businesses and small Indian casinos that had to have state gambling licenses. The two bandits were a white male and black male in their mid-thirties. They wore ball caps, hoodies and dark sunglasses when they walked into the camera view. Their take-over cowboy-style of robbery was dramatic and frightening for the patrons, and incredibly dangerous to boot. The fact that no one had been killed, and only one security guard wounded, was a miracle. DOJ had run a computer analysis program on the crook's MO and found that it predicted a robbery in 3 days, which would be on a Friday in the early morning hours. The program couldn't predict where, other than in a 50-mile radius. They could pull quite a few of their own agents for the detail but it wasn't nearly enough to put the desired three officers on every potential target. The supervising special agent wanted three officers because there were two crooks and he wasn't sure if they had a wheel man added to the mix. The commanders reached agreement on which sites would be covered by whom and what time the operation would start and stop. It appeared that most of the logistics were covered. The DOJ supervisor added one little twist that instantly pissed off Sergeant Glen. He wanted at least one of his people on the most likely target sites. The supervisor said that this was to maintain investigative continuity with all the previous work that had been done, but Bud and everybody else knew that was not the real reason.

The old Bud Glen would have immediately jumped down this guy's throat and called him on his bullshit, but Bud was older and wiser now and thought he'd try to do this the polite way, even if he did feel like one of those coat and tie pussies from administration. Bud looked at Lieutenant Jenkins and half raised his hand signaling that he had a comment. For a minute Bud thought the Lieutenant was going to ignore him, which the Lieutenant thought about doing, but eventually he said, "Bud, did you have a comment?"

"Ya Lieutenant, I see a problem mixing personnel who haven't worked together and aren't even from the same agency. Policy and tactical differences could create confusion and in a takedown like this with heavily armed suspects. We don't need extra problems. I recommend we place DOJ staffed stakeout teams at strategic points throughout the county so they can respond to any site before we notify the media or crime scene people. They can still manage the investigation and take over the case." Bud reminded himself to shut up and not say another word if he met resistance. He was also quite proud of himself for not once referring to anyone as a "Media Whore."

Lieutenant Jenkins was visibly relieved when Bud finished. He looked at the DOJ supervisor and said, "I think Bud makes a good point. You and I can make up the staffing order after the meeting. No need to have everybody sit through that." The DOJ guy just nodded his agreement and Jenkins dismissed everybody with a sigh of relief.

Sergeant Glen pulled in almost the whole gang squad (sixteen officers) and told them they'd be pulling some stake out duty Friday night so they needed to get some sleep.

He reminded them that these 211pc guys were the real deal so they needed to be rested and alert. Bobby and Cam were assigned an Indian Casino along with Erin, one of the two female squad members. This place had a high Hispanic patronage so they thought her Spanish language skills might come in handy. The casino was little more than a glorified motel with a big gambling hall, but it did have its own security force consisting of three people tonight, which helped the officers set up a good surveillance post. There were a lot of tactical issues to working in an environment like this. Any actions you took had to consider the huge number of citizens that could be hurt in a shoot-out. The security officers were largely kids and retired guys with minimal training, and while they wanted to be helpful, they could be a liability if something went down. Cam told the security supervisor that he needed a portable radio so he could talk with their people in an emergency and made it clear in a quick briefing that the odds were nothing would happen here tonight. But if it did he expected them to follow his instructions. They were all cooperative and seemed glad to have professional help. Cam, Bobby, and Erin all set up in an office adjacent to the money room and watched the whole casino on closed circuit television. This location had good access to a number of escape routes and would allow Cam and company several routes to intercept robbers if they should hit this place.

The tactical approach on an assignment like this was to put plain clothes people on site and let the crime go down. A few political critics didn't like that enforcement tactic. They thought the crime should be stopped before it occurred. It was the classic "Prevention vs. Enforcement" argument. It was always desirable to stop a crime before it occurred, but it was tough to get a conviction in many cases unless you let it go down and proved that the crooks were really going to rob the place. The issue here was, "What was safer for the public?" And the answer was: let it happen, and arrest the crooks away from the casino. Trying to arrest them before it went down would likely hurt patrons and might result in a failed prosecution.

The officers settled in for long night. Erin borrowed some playing cards and told Bobby she would show him how the other 95% lived. They kept one eye on the monitor but knew that Cam was on point while they played cards.

Cam started to fill the time after three hours of butt numbing stakeout with "crazy cop" stories. He asked Bobby and Erin if they ever worked with Steve Bishop from Mountain View. Both of them said no, but Erin had heard of him because he was a good athlete and won several medals in the Police and Fire Summer Games. Cam explained that Mountain View always got run over by San Jose P.D. in the games just because of San Jose's size and that it always pissed off Steve when he had to hear how many medals San Jose won while Mountain View's count was always weenie. One of the guys that dished out the crap was Erin's partner Todd, who was frequently described by her as "Igor" or the "missing link."

One morning, while a bunch of the guys from both departments were eating breakfast in a café on the highway between the two cities called "Momma's Place," Steve drove up in his marked unit and saw that Todd was there. He knew that Todd couldn't resist handing out a ration of crap about the recent Summer Games, so he hatched a plot. He got his Slim Jim door opener out of his car and popped the car door on Todd's marked unit. He put his tool back in his car then reached into Todd's. He grabbed Todd's radio mic and ripped its wire cord loose from the base, and then put it, long tail and all, in his jacket pocket. As he walked into the café past Todd, Todd made a wise crack about the Summer Games.

Steve stopped and said, "Hey Todd, I think you got a call on your radio."

Todd replied, "I have a portable and I didn't hear anything."

Steve then handed him his Mic with the cord dangling and said, "Try this one and see if it works," as he walked on. Todd was silent for almost a minute while everyone around him was busting up laughing.

He walked up to Steve with mic in hand with the cord dangling at his side and said, "How the fuck am I supposed to explain this?"

Steve shrugged and said, "Well, whatever you do I won't tell them that you left your car unlocked." Todd was very confused and couldn't remember if he locked his car or not, so he just walked off mumbling.

Erin was laughing at this story so hard she almost fell out of her chair. "You'd have to work with him to appreciate how much that screwed with his sense of world order."

Bobby said, "Okay, I got one for you. This lunatic I went through the academy with worked for El Dorado County Sheriff's Department. He and his partner always noticed that this very difficult Captain was always watching the Deputies start their marked units on the day shift through his office window to see if they were doing anything he could ding them for. This Deputy found that on his old patrol car, the RPM's, when it was cold, would run so fast that if you put the car in gear and set the emergency brake the car would gallop forward about six inches every couple of seconds. So, one day he brought a flake of hay from his barn at home, and pulled the car up so the Captain could see it. He popped the hood so it was open about a foot and proceeded to feed the car hay into the open engine hood as he walked backwards and the car followed him without a driver. When he got to the end of the driveway he shut the hood and drove away. He got called back to the station about 20 minutes later where the Sheriff and Captain were waiting for him. He said he'd almost convinced the Sheriff that the Captain was having a breakdown if they hadn't found some hay in the driveway."

Laughing, Bobby said, "Okay Cam, you're up."

Cam thought for a moment and said, "This is a classic. You guys remember Phil the silver haired guy that retired two years ago?" They both nodded. "Well he was one of my training officers and one night when I came to work he made me do everything that shift because he'd been in court all day for eight hours and had a full shift to go. He was tired, old, and grumpy. We got a call from the burger joint down on 16th street, run by the Russian guy who never bathes or washes anything in his business. This guy was always having problems with the health department, and with his customers about their orders not being right, or them getting tired of waiting and leaving. So, we get this call about the customer refusing to pay because the order was wrong, and when we explained to the owner that people didn't have to pay for something they didn't order he started swearing and threw the food at our feet. I'm sure he picked it up and served to someone else later. Phil just closed his notebook and walked away. As I drove the unit down the street I could tell he was doing a slow boil, but since I was in training I thought it best to keep quiet. After about four hours went by, he had me pull into a gas station that had a pay phone. He put in some money and made a call while I stood beside our car. He hung up and waited a couple of minutes and the phone rang. He answered it, talked for just a second and then said, "Okay let's drive." About an hour later dispatch sent us back to the burger joint because someone made a fictitious order claiming to be a church youth field trip, for 35 burgers, 25 orders of fries, and 30 Cokes. Apparently, the call back number used to confirm the order was a pay phone and not the church.

When the Russian, who was foaming at the mouth, asked why shit like this was always happening to him, and what he was supposed to do with all this food Phil said, "You could try not being such an asshole," and then recommended he give the food to the homeless shelter down the street.

After he got in the car he looked at me with a serious face and said, "This was an example of unprofessional conduct and I don't ever want to see you pulling crap like that." So, I drove and didn't say a word.

Cam pointed his finger at Bobby and then Erin.

Erin said, "Okay I've got a goody I almost forgot about. Cam's story reminded me of one about my training officer Al Sylvester. Al was a veteran cop with experience at a couple of different agencies before he came here. The other places he worked were on the east coast near New York and New Jersey so he had a little different take on law enforcement. He was famous for doing a lot, and I mean a lot, of personal business on duty, but in all fairness when he was a detective he did a lot of investigative work on his off time. A slimy cop by the name of Bob Jonas married Al's ex-wife and was jealous of Al's detective job so he burned him with Internal Affairs about all the on-duty personal errands. Rumor was that Al's ex wasn't finding his replacement as good in the bedroom so that added to the motive to hurt Al. Anyway, Internal Affairs did an investigation and alleged that Al did some banking, got a haircut and watched his kid's ball game while on duty."

"At the personnel review hearing where they looked at how much punishment he was going to get, the six people who were on the board asked Sylvester what he had to say about the accusations and Al smiled and shrugged as he said, "I earned the money while I was on duty so I figured I might as well bank it on duty and my hair grows on duty so I figured I might as well get it trimmed while I was on duty. As far as watching my kid's ball game, I conceived that kid while I was on duty so.........well you get it, I'm sure."

"The whole personnel board busted up laughing, and when they were done they composed themselves and gave Al a three-day suspension without pay. The normal punishment would have been two weeks but they liked him and also the fact that he didn't come to the hearing and deny the charges or snivel. The brass upstairs didn't find him quite so charming and transferred him out of detectives and back to patrol where he didn't have as much freedom to screw around. The detective lieutenant was pissed and told the brass that they just transferred the best dick he's ever had and that they'd see a decline in the closure rate the next month."

After they all stopped laughing, Bobby took over the camera-watching duties.

As he looked at the gambling patrons through the very high-resolution camera that allowed you to zoom in and out at will he commented, "This casino could use a little drug influence enforcement. A lot of these folks look like spaced out zombies."

Erin smiled and said, "Bobby, video poker all night long and meth freaks are a marriage made in heaven. Not only does it make the casino serious money and keep cranksters off the street but it recycles welfare dollars back into the city as taxable income. Sometimes it's best not to screw with natural adaptation."

Bobby smiled at her and asked, "Is Todd rubbing off on you, Erin?"

Just then Bobby got deadly serious and said, "Hey guys, we got two males who fit the description and they look nervous." Cam and Erin looked over Bobby's shoulder at the monitor. Instantly everyone's heart rate doubled. The two suspects were wearing long dark trench coats and were holding something underneath them. The clothing didn't fit the weather or gambling environment. All of the officers watching felt sure that this was a robbery about to go down. Cam remembered the training video on the Miami FBI shoot out that occurred decades ago, with two heavily armed bank robbers and decided he wouldn't make the same mistake of going it alone.

He hit Sergeant Glen on his portable using a secure frequency and said, "S7, this is unit 22."

Glen answered, "Go ahead 22."

"Sarg, we got a possible that fits the description to a tee and they're checking everything out like they're about ready to hit it. Stand by for confirmation."

Glen said, "Copy."

As soon as the guns came out Cam keyed his radio mic and said, "S7, it's going down. Send the cavalry."

Glen said, "Copy 22, we're in route." Cam turned down the radio and pocketed it. Bobby and Erin looked at him since he was the senior guy in charge and waited for his instructions. Everybody's adrenaline was pumping and heart rates were at their max.

Cam said, "We need to let it go down since there are so many civilians around. No way we can take them down here without shooting innocents. If we try to box them in the money room we'll launch a hostage situation. We'll see which escape route they use and follow. When we get our break, we'll engage them but not till its right. At some point, they'll get in a car and then we'll have some containment. They have a rifle and a shotgun tonight so keep that in mind if we get into a gun battle. Our body armor won't stop rifle rounds." Cam now had to decide whether or not to let the security officers know about this event. If he had a hotdog working tonight who wanted to be a hero it could backfire to tell him but he quickly decided that once he had a direction of flight he'd notify the security officers. He couldn't live with himself if one of them got shot because he withheld information. The crooks had two clerks lying face down in the cashier's booth and were screaming for the one standing clerk to hurry up and fill the money bag. At times like this, cops prayed the crooks were not frightened or strung out on drugs because cool professional crooks kill fewer people. Panicked amateurs are dangerous. The crooks had obviously cased the place prior and knew exactly when an employee with a collection cart was due to enter the money exchange room. That allowed them access to the heavily fortified office.

Bobby and Erin checked their shotguns and Cam watched to see which exit they would use. Cam said, "Stand by. We're about to hit it." The stickup men exited the front of the money exchange after spending less than 90 seconds gathering up cash. They fled toward the south exit which dumped right into the ground level of a three-story parking garage. As Cam and the others left their surveillance room Cam used his other casino portable radio to broadcast instruction to the already alerted security officers. He told them the crooks were exiting south and headed to the parking lot.

He said, "Don't engage them; there are too many civilians in the way. Assume a cover position at the lot entrance and wait for them to try to exit." He instructed security to use their units to block the exit and admonished them to not break cover because the suspects had a high-power rifle. Cam reasoned that if he and his two partners couldn't get it done, security could shoot the crap out of the crooks as they tried to flee. Just inside the garage structure Cam saw a light blue Buick which had been mentioned in the briefing as a possible vehicle used by the crooks. It was running, parked in a narrow slot just past the first driving lane into the structure as the lane curved up toward the second level.

Cam grabbed Erin by the arm and said, "Erin, take those stairs to the second level and shoot down on the engine and tires to disable their car. Hurry!" She peeled off and approached the stairs at a dead run. As she got to the stairs a young casino security guard appeared coming from the other direction.

She wasn't quite sure what to do with him and assumed he didn't hear Cam's broadcasted instructions, so she said, "You, you're with me" as she pointed with her left hand to her side. The kid fell in as ordered. Cam had radioed in their location to Sergeant Glen and he and Bobby assumed cover behind a six-foot-wide concrete pillar that held up a portion of the garage. Their location was 25 yards behind the suspect's car with a clear view. The crooks had gotten into the back seat and the car was getting ready to depart when Erin and her new sidekick opened up on it. They were both on their knees to get some cover from the three-foot concrete retaining wall. When they had arrived, Erin told the kid with her to shoot his .357 Smith & Wesson revolver at the bottom of the two tires they could see on their side of the car. She figured if he shot low the rounds would deflect off the concrete, up into the tire. She opened up on the engine assuming that if she put enough 00 Buck into the engine compartment she'd destroy at least some of the electronics necessary to make the car run.

As Cam and Bobby watched the driver, who they later would find out was a girlfriend of one of the bandits, put the car in reverse and start to back out, all hell broke loose. Six rounds from the hand gun and four rounds from the shotgun brought the car to a dead stop with two flat tires and a dead engine. All the people in the car laid down on the seats because they assumed the cops were shooting to kill them not to disable the car.

Cam, seeing this said, "Bobby, one round through the back window for effect." Bobby squeezed off a round out of his shotgun disintegrating the window. Cam then yelled to the crooks, "Police. Drop your guns and get your hands where I can see them." Before the crooks could respond five marked units dropped into the garage and spread out in a semi-circle behind the suspect car.

Cam said over his portable to the marked units, "This is unit 22, marked unit you have the stop," which meant they were in charge of giving the crooks instructions. In situations like this, where marked units and plain clothed detectives are working together, it's best to let the uniformed officers take the lead if nothing unusual is occurring because it's easy to confuse cops and crooks. The first unit to arrive which centered up behind the Buick got out of his car and squatted behind the door. He had turned his car slightly to the left to get some protection from the engine block and was talking to the crooks over his outside radio speaker. Every other cop at the scene had his weapon out and had picked a target in the event of gunfire. It would have been an exceedingly stupid move for the suspects to fire a round. This is often the message law enforcement wants to send to crooks. It stops violence because most people, when faced with overwhelming odds, give up.

"Occupants of the car drop your guns and get your hands in the air so I can see them." It took a while for the robbers to respond but after a little thought they assumed they wouldn't survive a shootout with a dozen guns aimed at them from a variety of directions, especially since they were in a car that didn't work anymore. The marked unit had them get out one at a time and walk backwards toward the officers. They were told to lie down on the ground with their hands out to their sides and wait. When all three were proned out on the driveway a couple of officers cautiously approached the car to make sure it was empty, then they cuffed the crooks.

As Sergeant Glen and the DOJ supervisor arrived to look things over, Erin walked up with her new security officer buddy in tow. She looked at Sergeant Glen and said, "If you're looking for any new officers to hire I've a good candidate for you" and nodded toward the kid. She patted him on the shoulder and started to walk off to join Cam and Bobby.

Sergeant Glen said, "Erin, whose idea was it to disable that car from the second deck?"

"Cam the man. Pretty slick huh?" Glen nodded his head in agreement.

INFESTATION IS HARD TO CURE

J-Tra and the boys were making pretty good progress toward expansion of their criminal enterprise. They had recruited two street whores into their operation by strong arming them and supplying them with a hassle-free source for meth. The carrot and the stick worked in a great many settings. They were programing two younger girls who weren't whores yet, but that would come with time. They also expanded into more auto theft. Car rip-offs had multiple value because they were good for several crimes. They could use a car in a robbery or burglary because the plates wouldn't come back to them, and then take it to an out of town chop shop that would dismantle it for the parts. If you were lucky some chump left some valuable stuff in the car like electronics or gifts during the holidays. The gang figured out it was too risky to steal the cars themselves because the cops had too many bait cars in operation and it was a 50/50 shot of being nabbed for the crime. J-Tra knew this from personal experience. That's how he got his prison sentence, so they used strung-out tweakers. They gave them a small taste of crank, then would tell them to rip certain vehicles and meet at another location where they would get the rest of the meth. Sometime the cranksters were given shaved keys or other tools to help in the rip off. They also made it clear that if they told the cops they were stealing on consignment that bad things would happen to them and their families.

∞

The gang enforcement squad was brutally aware that all this criminal action was taking its toll on the city. The victimless crimes of narcotics and vice were racking up a lot of victims. Junkies and speed freaks were ripping off people to support their habit. If citizens got in the way, they sometimes got hurt. Thefts and burglaries became assaults or worse when people resisted. Johns and their wives were getting exposed to diseases. Young girls were been recruited into a life of drugs and prostitution. New gang bangers were failing at school, and fear among the law-abiding citizens was growing daily. Huge portions of the city, like parks and shopping centers, were so thug-infested that they were virtually off limits to families. Security guards at grocery stores is a 21st-century evolution. Not to mention lost opportunities for a generation of kids. Social devolution was in full swing. The country was abandoning stable government and reverting to tribal warfare. When a buddy was shot in a drive-by you didn't talk to the cops. You took care of it yourself. The streets of Fallujah ran through Norman Rockwell's America.

It was a lot like a cockroach infestation and the cure was almost as harmful as the original problem. The only thing that worked in a democratic society with constitutional rights was a quasi-police-state of gang injunctions and police crash units. This caused problems for everyone, especially minority citizens, who got lumped in with the crooks and who were often the victims of their own people. Crime in this country is often, caused by an ethnic group victimizing its own people. Sergeant Glen often paralleled gang infestation to a toxic industry that pollutes the air, the water, and the ground, damaging all the children who lived there with poison sludge. After the entire area is uninhabitable, those that can, move on. The poor, the young and the old are stuck.

∞

Sergeant Glen was trying to explain this infestation to a group of parents at a high school "meet and greet" the chief had delegated him to attend. He often thought that assignments like this were payback for his irreverence.

To illustrate the dilemma about parenting, gangs, culture and family, he told them the story of John Fernandez, who was a patrol Captain at his agency.

John and his wife Socorro had two kids, a boy and girl who had entered their teens in the city of San Jose. They were bright, loving children who enjoyed family outings and the company of their parents until the teenage years and peer pressure started to take hold. They both had started to be rude, detached, constantly plugged into some type of technology and, worst of all, they started hanging around dirt bags who dressed like thugs and whores. Eventually their grades in school started to decline and they hid out in their rooms when they were forced to be home.

John's wife also worked for the P.D. as a civilian employee in the records division and she helped as an interpreter when needed. She got to see firsthand what happened when kids started sliding down that slippery slope. All her aspirations of seeing her children go to college and having a tight family relationship seemed to be in jeopardy. She was raised in a large, connected, loving family and wanted hers to be the same way.

One night, when she and John were home alone and sipping a glass of wine on their patio she told John about all her fears and then she cried and said, "John we're losing our children to this street culture and I'm scared to death."

John said, "I know, and I've been worried about it too."

As they sat together looking up at the stars John reminded himself that his best ideas came when he didn't wallow in the details but stepped back and analyzed the big picture. He knew his wife well, as they had been through a lifetime of struggle and work together, so he knew he needed to approach her correctly. He had an idea but it had to be presented gently and allow her to buy in at her own speed.

"I have an idea but it's going to require you to be brave and do something that you'll hate."

Frightened, she said, "What?"

John asked, "Would your parents take the kids for a year?" He sat quietly starring at the night sky and waited.

She was breathless for a moment and slowly when she realized what John had in mind, she nodded her head as she started to cry again because she knew it needed to happen, even though she'd be heartbroken not having the kids live with them for a whole year. She also knew that she wouldn't witness their ascension into adulthood.

Her parents were old school Mexicans who lived south of Guadalajara. Her Dad was a building contractor who employed a dozen men and Mom was traditional as they come. No one gave Dad any guff and you were expected to work when you ate his food and lived in his house. Girls were chaperoned on dates until they decided the boy could be trusted and clothing was modest and proper. Technology was very limited, simply as a rule of courtesy. John and Socorro were planning Christmas with her parents in a few weeks so they called them and told them their idea. The parents agreed and after a few days at the parents' house John and his wife broke it to the kids and hopped a plane back to the U. S. They also took the kids' clothes and toys with them.

After a flurry of phone calls and emotional meltdowns the kids accepted their fate and, after a few months, started to adapt. John and his wife would visit on a holiday or two but the kids were told they had to do a year to experience the Mexican culture as it truly was and learn the language that would expand their career opportunities. The results were astounding. The kids became truly multicultural and developed a sense of what was important in life and what wasn't. All the childish peer group obsession dropped away.

This type of tactical intervention is called a "Bold Adjustment" in Army artillery battalions. If you're missing the target by a lot, don't make incremental adjustments. Throw away your previous plan and recalculate to hit your target. Sometimes parenting requires a Bold Adjustment.

After a year when John was ready to bring the kids home his son asked to stay a little longer because Grandpa had him working as a foreman on an important construction project and the money was good. When they all finally arrived home John's wife cried one more time because she truly had her children back and enjoyed the young adults they had become. John's daughter actually thanked her parents for giving her a chance to know her grandparents on a level that most children never experience. The kids became people John and his wife liked as well as loved. Not all parents can say that.

Sergeant Glen pointed out that what happened in Mexico to these kids was a cultural experience. What happens in a barrio gang banger's life is a "criminal subculture" that has nothing to do with being Hispanic. Hating ghetto culture was not the same thing as hating Hispanics. Sergeant Glen hoped this message would spread but, a cynic at heart, he doubted it. People like to generalize and it was in fact a survival technique, a type of mental code that lets you decide quickly if you should be fearful or not. And when young guys dressed and acted like thugs to be cool it was human nature to judge them as dangerous. You had to be young and hip to tell the difference between cool and criminal. Even then, it wasn't always easy, especially when many young people had one foot in both worlds.

The downside to these community meetings was that Sergeant Glen would often get heat about the latest police shooting. He was always tempted to get into specifics, but that would require a level of knowledge about the law and tactical procedure that citizens just don't have. He also knew that some citizens' opinions were often based on emotion, or an internet video and occasionally a deep prejudice against police that rivaled the prejudice of any Klansman's. The public simply wasn't used to seeing force used on someone. It's almost always ugly. They thought women and teenagers should get a free pass because they didn't understand that women and teenagers are just as deadly and violent as men. They thought cops all knew Kung Fu and that the original charge was relevant after the suspect started resisting arrest. They just didn't understand the rules of the profession and they didn't want to treat each incident of force with due process. They wanted to judge officers collectively, just like racists judge minorities.

So, Glen just gave his standard explanation of policing in America:

"There are about 800,000 officers in the United States spread throughout 18,000 agencies and they make somewhere between 35,000 and 40,000 arrests every day. They operate in the most violent anti-authority western culture there is, where hillbillies everywhere loved that Johnny Paycheck song "Take This Job and Shove it" and let's not forget how the inmates cheered when Johnny Cash sang, "But I shot a man in Reno just to watch him die." This is all done in a country that has at least one million heroin addicts, a million cocaine addicts, a million and a half meth users and God know how many PCP and acid freaks. Add in the pot heads, and alcoholics and that subtotal will be dwarfed by the prescription drug addicts. Don't forget we have gangs in every city in the country and they're in possession of some of the most lethal firearms amongst the 350,000,000 guns in our borders ever made to fight wars with. The fact that we're not stacking up bodies every morning like cord wood is a testament to the sacrifice and discipline of United States Law Enforcement officers everywhere. Most people, when they travel abroad, wouldn't dare pull the crap in a foreign country that they pull here. Ninety percent of other countries on this planet shoot you for running away from an officer, let alone swinging on a cop. If we armed all the complainers and had them do police work for one day, America would experience its first modern holocaust."

This caustic rant usually stopped further questions about police abuse but Sergeant Glen doubted it changed too many minds. But Glen being Glen would settle for the silence.

∞

Speaking of rants, J-Tra was pissed. When Jose got pantsed in front of all those school kids the word spread fast and it brought recruitment to a screeching halt. It also humiliated the gang. He went on a hour long rant that scared even his closest friends that night at the gang house. They all knew that J-Tra was capable of extreme violence because they'd seen him beat other gang members nearly to death with little provocation.

"That mother fucking pig can't dis us like that. And what did you do about it, José, you pussy? You just walked away without jumping him. You make me sick, man. For the next month, you don't come in this house unless you're wearing a bra. You gonna act like a little bitch you'll dress like one." The final sentence in his speech was punctuated by a wine bottle across the side of Jose's head.

As Ray was telling Cam and Bobby the details of this story he looked at Cam and said, "J-Tra wants you dead man. And he's putting so much heat on Jose, that I think he'll take a shot at you if he gets a chance. I mean wearing a bra is like the most cold thing I've ever seen done to a homie. He like wears this bra on the outside of his shirt when he has to be in the house. Mostly he doesn't come around but when he has to, he gets nothing but shit from the other guys. All he talks about is paying you back for what you did to him."

Cam said, "Good to know. Thanks, Ray."

Bobby could see that Cam took it seriously, but what really impressed him was that Ray was willing to share the information knowing that if it leaked out it would mean his death. Bobby believed, without a doubt, that Ray wasn't headed down the gang road anymore and that he really wanted to get away from them.

∞

J-Tra was angry but, after cooling down, he had to look at the plus side of things. He had two new whores almost ready for the street. One was a little rich bitch who was rebelling against her daddy's strict rules and the other was a forgotten victim of divorce who just fell through the family cracks. Both had been partying hard with the gang and got introduced to some serious dope. Ecstasy was a good way to break in a whore because when people used it they became uninhibited and craved physical contact. Videos and pictures were taken as the very drugged girls engaging in a five hour sex party and they were already shown to the girls as a reminder that they couldn't go back to their old friends and family who wouldn't understand. The psychological down from ecstasy made the offer of some laced marijuana sound good. Their boyfriends didn't bother to explain the black tar heroin part of their high. They just told them that it was primo weed. A few more weeks of this smoke and they'd be smoking the tar straight. A few months later a needle and syringe full of heroin wouldn't seem like a big leap. If they fought you upping their drug use or you were in a hurry you could lock them down and inject them with heroin. These two new girls probably were going to be force-fed dope because J-Tra was in a hurry. Soon they wouldn't mind. The good thing about getting whores strung out on heroin is that they could still function half way well and didn't look bad for a few years, unlike meth. Meth would burn up a user in months and they could barely keep it together long enough to turn a decent trick.

∞

J-Tra would need to find a couple of new crew members though. Two of his boys got picked up for a drive-by shooting. A rival gang was sniffing around their turf and had to be scared off. The two guys that did the shooting violated a solid rule. They didn't ditch the hot car they were driving fast enough and a patrol cop spotted them. There was a chase where they crashed their ride and got caught, guns and all.

To top off all the problems J-Tra was dealing with right now, he had to find Dory and get her dropped off at Manny's house. Manny was getting to be a serious problem because he kept demanding more of Dory's time and he was pressuring J-Tra for more money. What the stupid fuck didn't get was that Dory was a source of money, but she couldn't make money if she was with Manny all the time and he couldn't use her if Manny beat the crap out of her and she was so bruised up and cut she couldn't turn tricks.

Dory was a textbook case of the slow slide into the drug lifestyle. She started using gateway drugs like pot and pills with her sisters and their boyfriends. They were a few years older than she was so she thought they were cool and didn't want to appear scared or too young to party with them. When you're 13 and stoned the older guys take advantage of you. Dory lost her virginity, her purse, and her self-respect at a party one night where her sister was too screwed up to notice. Dory thought smoking heroin on a piece of tin foil (they call it chasing the dragon) wasn't going to get her addicted. She was wrong. It only took about two weeks and she moved to the needle.

Like all new users, she believed that if her drug use was getting out of control she would just go cold turkey and quit. The problem was she didn't understand the nature of addiction. It destroys that part of your willpower that allows you control. Most female heroin addicts will eventually turn to prostitution. They all say they'd rather be sick from withdrawal, but once they're strung out they start turning tricks. Dory was no different. Eventually she did what all addicts do, which is any crime available and easy. Shoplifting and refunding was good for some quick cash. As long as she looked like a respectable soccer mom she could steal clothes and return them for cash. The merchants didn't want to piss off a customer, so she could pull it off a couple times per store before they told her no. She registered for community college and got student loans but never attended past the first week. Writing checks and identity theft were good scams. If you got caught, the sentence was always local time or probation. When all else failed you simply went up to a house and rang the bell. If someone answered you asked for a fictitious person. If no one answered you opened the gate and broke into the back. Rural ranchers were easy marks because they had lots of tools and equipment that could be hawked for dope money. They couldn't watch their barn and home every waking hour. Lately she had to let these other scams go because J-Tra was working her so much there wasn't any time and the last few months he'd been loaning her to his boss Manny. When she complained to him about the beatings J-Tra said he couldn't tell the Nuestra Familia shot caller no or he'd have some serious problems. She hated Manny Salinas and had fantasies about shooting his drunken smelly fat ass.

∞

Cam, Bobby and the other gang unit officers were putting serious heat on J-Tra and a few other area gangs, but like all good businesses the gangs just worked harder to overcome the setbacks. Dope was the fallback action when the cops got too aggressive. Stealing cars and doing burglaries was not as good an option because too much was out of your control. With dope, you could set up buys out of town or use a cut out, someone that was expendable to mule the dope to the buyer. If you sold to a narc you lost some money but it was just part of the drill, because most buys weren't for that much dope. If you lost a gang member to the joint, that was just the price of doing business. It was just "overhead." Besides it was a good way for a junior member to build his "cred's with the gang."

One of the dangers in policing is tunnel vision. You can't get so focused on one criminal organization that you neglect other groups that need attention. Sergeant Glen told the unit members at a briefing a few days ago to make sure they gave some of the other deserving citizens of their community a little police service. Bobby identified a particular group that investigation showed was up and coming. Their boss had served time for murder and assault and detectives believed he was responsible for taking a shot at a marked unit a couple of months ago. They didn't have enough proof to arrest him but believed a credible informant who identified the thug as the shooter.

From their undercover unit one night, Bobby and Cam were watching the leader of this black street gang that was trying to get traction in their city. The crook left his home all dressed up for a night on the town. He picked up a lady who was dressed up "ghetto fabulous" and they followed them to a local night spot favored by black gangsters. The crook pulled up to a side street near the club and sat in his car for a few minutes before going inside with his date.

As they watched Bobby said, "What do you suppose is the hang up here? Why aren't they going inside?"

"Because Bobby, they're doing a little dope and hiding their guns under the front seat. Did you see that muscle at the front door of the bar? The bouncers search all customers, men and women, before they go in. Too many shootings get you lots of police service."

Sure enough, after a few minutes the couple walked to the door where they were politely patted down, her purse was checked and they were allowed entrance. Cam told Bobby to drive around the block and park a half a block behind the crook's older model classic Cadillac. He produced a "Slim Jim" door opening tool from under the front set of their undercover Mustang and got out. Cops learned a great deal from repossesers and tow companies. There's a tool to open any car door.

Bobby was shaking his head and muttered under his breath, "Here we go again."

Cam popped the door in seconds and slid into the driver's seat, extinguishing the interior light. He found two guns under the front seat. A Colt model 19, .45 caliber automatic and obviously the lady's piece, a .32 caliber revolver made by some company he'd never heard of. He also found a baggy with a healthy amount of coke in it. He pocketed everything but the coke then started cramming wads of paper and a couple of tooth picks he found into the ignition key slot of the Cadillac. He took his knife out and locked the blade where upon he proceeded to pack all the debris in the ignition till he couldn't fill it anymore. He got out and locked the car and sprinkled the coke all over the front wind shield. The evening dew would do the rest.

As he got back into the Mustang Bobby asked, "What did you find?"

Cam said, "Nothing much. The usual."

Bobby figured that if he wanted to talk about it he would. Cam often did stuff like this and trying to debate the ethics of it was pointless.

Cam knew the stuff he found on an illegal search couldn't be used in court but he hated the idea of a thug and his woman driving away with guns that could be used to kill a cop, so he eliminated the criminal contraband. His tactics were born out of frustration. There were so many of these thug lowlifes packing guns and using dope that most cops just got some justice anyway they could. The criminal justice system had become a joke. The issue wasn't, "Did someone break the law?" anymore. It was "Did you catch them fairly." What he also knew was that crooks had a problem reporting themselves victims of a crime when the property taken was illegal.

Cam smiled as he thought of those two loaded dirt bags trying to start their ride at the end of the night and finding their car didn't work and all their shit was gone.

∞

The next day, Bobby told Cam that it was time to try to contact the two women they had IDed from the search warrant material they seized. All their other assignments and stakeout activities had hit a lull. They pulled together everything they could find on the women and tried to plan the best place to talk to them that would lend itself to the ladies being cooperative.

Judy Beckett was living with another street hooker in a flop house near the freeway, so contacting her at home was not a good idea. When you were asking someone to rat on their pimp or gang members it was best to keep it a private conversation. They figured it was a good idea to catch her on the street and take her to a park for a beer and some talk. This required some surveillance but eventually they timed it right.

As she was walking down a busy city street Bobby waited till a couple of homeless guys walked by before he jumped out of the car, IDed himself and asked her to take a ride. She was a bit freaked out because she'd been busted before and this wasn't how cops did it, but she guessed she didn't have much choice but to go along. Bobby looked through her purse quickly to make sure she wasn't packing and noticed a bunch of condoms and some drug paraphernalia before he handed it back. When they got to the park and everybody but Bobby had their beer they began to ask her how she got into the business. She didn't want to talk about it, but eventually came clean with a brief story that blamed mostly herself for just giving up and getting into the dope life style. When Cam started to gently mention helping them get information on the gang and J-Tra she immediately shut Cam down.

She said, "That's suicide and you'll never get him." She reached out and unconsciously touched a scar that ran from the top of her ear to her jaw bone, that Cam was sure was J-Tra's work.

When it became obvious that she wasn't going to work with them, Bobby told her that they would give her a lift back down town and that she probably didn't want to mention that she talked with the cops because J-Tra might misunderstand and he was paranoid enough to think she was a snitch. When they dropped her off Bobby told her that if she ever needed help to call him that she was a victim and not the people he and Cam were after. She just nodded and walked away.

"One down and batting zero" said Bobby.

"How about Guadalupe Diaz, Bobby? What's our plan of attack on today's second rejection?"

"Let's swing over to her street. It's not too far from here and I have her cell number. I teased it out of some department data banks for the vice detail."

As they rounded the corner Bobby dialed her number and when she answered, using his best Mexican accent, he said, "Chica, I think somebody hit your parked car." Then he killed the call. A few seconds later she stepped out her door in a big hurry and walked over to a broken-down Toyota with an off colored driver's door. As she walked around the car looking at it she looked up to find Bobby smiling.

He showed her his badge and told her, "Your car's fine. I just wanted you out of the house so we could talk. Come with us please." As he opened the door for her she got in but was obviously frightened. She looked too young to drink beer so they just walked through the park and sat at a picnic table. She took an instant liking to Bobby so Cam just let Bobby do the talking. Bobby was good at meeting people for the first time. There was something about his easy smile and light sense of humor that made him approachable. People forgot he was a cop and opened up to him, where other officer had trouble making that connection. Lupe was surprisingly candid and had not lost enough of her old self to give up her anger. She hated what the gang had done to her and the loss of her family's love made her cry. Bobby played it cool and didn't ask for anything firm right now but told her she had a friend and that he'd be there if she needed someone. He wrote down his undercover contact number at the PD and told her that they would talk some more later.

As he got ready to let her out of the car around the corner from her house Bobby took her hand in both of his and gave it a gentle squeeze as he said, "Lupe, I want you to think about what you want your life to look like a few months from now. Nothing's impossible you know." As she got out of the car she just stared at Bobby as they drove away.

Cam said, "I swear to 'Hey Zeus' you're a smooth-talking son of bitch, Officer Wright. I was almost ready to make love to you myself. She's gonna work with you. I'd bet serious money on it."

Bobby just smiled and nodded his head. He knew that relationships can't be forced and that people want to believe in something. Too many cops are impatient and don't let informants come around at their own speed. He believed it would work because hope is hard to kill, even the heart of a strung-out whore.

∞

While Bobby and Cam were working on turning informants the rest of the gang unit hadn't been sitting on their thumbs. A certified crazy man by the man of Todd Wilms had worked up a search warrant on J-Tra's car and house.

Not his gang crash pad but his family home where his mom, sister and brother lived.

Wilms was not a subtle cop. He was a 6-foot 3-inch weightlifter who took enough Creatine and supplements to make even the best liver work overtime. He was so strong that his muscles had their own muscles. And while he smiled a lot, it would be an error to think of him as gentle or nice.

When one of the younger squad members asked him why he didn't get some bad ass tattoo on his huge arms he replied, "You don't put clip art on a Rembrandt, Junior."

His warrant was based on a covered buy. He had sent an informant to buy drugs from J-Tra's little brother. "Borracho" was Rueben's street name because he drank too much. J-Tra had allowed his little brother to hang with the gang but at 17 he kept him away from the stuff that might get him hurt or busted seriously. He was, however, grooming him to take over the number two position with the gang when he was older so that if J-Tra got busted and had to do some time he wouldn't get pushed out by some up and comer.

Borracho's orientation to gang life included his first sexual experience at the gang house.

His brother laughed and said, "Meho, what you need is a woman to show you the Crack of Dawn." And she did. Borracho was in love when he exited a well-used bedroom and gang prostitute. He had dreamed of this moment but a fat unattractive kid like him couldn't have imagined having sex with a woman like Dawn. He thought her forced smile and gentle touch were all because she liked him. He didn't notice that she didn't return his clumsy wet kisses or that she seemed to be forcing her thoughts on things other than where she was. She didn't hate Borracho. She hated his brother for what she was being forced to do. Borracho was just another trick. There was no sense in getting ugly or using an emasculating put down. This kid wasn't bright enough to even understand.

Borracho felt that he could save Dawn from being shared with other men if he could gain some leverage or power. His brother just laughed when Borracho asked him not to pimp out Dawn.

He told him, "Man up, Ese. You can't fall in love with every woman you fuck. In fact, you shouldn't fall in love with any women you fuck."

Borracho wanted money to take Dawn on a real date so he started using his gang connections to deal a little weed on the side. He sold to Wilm's informant once, but that was before patrol had picked up the informant for shoplifting. A petty charge like this usually wouldn't be a problem and the informant would have been cited out, but he was too drunk to release and he had several earlier arrests for theft and burglary. Wilms recognized the informants' name when he was looking through the previous night's arrests. He'd busted him for some minor charges a few months back and knew he was a neighbor of J-Tra's family. Wilms made him an offer he couldn't refuse. He told him he would make all the shoplifting charges go away and he could earn $100 bucks if he could get a buy in to J-Tra. But Wilms settled for the brother when the informant told him that Borracho was the best he could do because J-Tra hated him. So, Wilms settled for Borracho if the informant could make the buy go down in the family house so he could get to J-Tra. The frosting on the cake was that baby brother borrowed J-Tra's car to deliver the dope. Since the stake out relayed that Little Brother left the house at 3:00 p.m. and drove J-Tra's car to the park where the sale went down, the warrant could include both the house and car. This really was a legal way of getting into J-Tra's stuff without having a legal hook into him.

If nothing else, this search warrant would give J-Tra a formal introduction to Mr. Todd (I'll pinch your head off) Wilms. Wilm's partner, Erin Fuller, had put together a slick surveillance operation on the house. She found a U.S. Marine

Lieutenant that lived across the street and got his permission to park a surveillance van in his driveway for a few days. The idea was to hit the house and car when J-Tra was there and hope he was holding something interesting when it happened.

One of the gang unit secretaries who'd been assigned to monitor the down load from the surveillance camera mounted in the van saw activity at the house and notified Erin. She reviewed the tape and told Todd that all the principals were in the house so it was now or never.

When the warrant was served the whole family was just sitting down to Sunday dinner. J-Tra's mom was unaccustomed to police with guns, dogs and tactical armor forcing their way into her home. Everyone was rounded up and after the couch was searched they were seated in the living room with an officer to watch them. The males were cuffed for security and Todd read the family the warrant. Erin read the warrant again in Spanish so there couldn't be any legal games played later by defense attorneys claiming they didn't understand the warrant. Todd and Erin then did the same thing with the Miranda warning. After all the formalities Todd asked everyone who they were.

He asked J-Tra's sister, "Are you related to the family or are you one of J-Tra's prostitutes."

This was an insult that J-Tra and his sister found hard to take. They began swearing, saying there was no need to disrespect them this way. What they didn't know was that this was Todd's favorite pet peeve and he might have even set them up for a little couch education. He launched in to a speech about the term Respect and proceeded to explain to the J-Tra family about how real respect is earned.

He topped it off with a question. "Why do you feel that you are entitled to respect when you turn young girls into whores, deal drugs, shoot at people like cowards as you drive by them, and generally break laws and make neighborhoods violent cesspools of crime? Respect? There's nothing about you that I respect. You're just a stupid piece of criminal shit and all these family members are part of the problem because they tolerate it and use the money your crimes produce." Todd's eye contact with J-Tra's mom brought her to tears as she dealt with her own shame and guilt.

J-Tra was so angry he could barely control himself but he knew he was in no position to do anything about this insult now. All he could do was choke it down and swear he'd pay this pig back soon. He couldn't believe these gang unit cops. They were becoming a huge problem. They didn't follow rules, they insulted his family and were blocking his business at every turn, and now they were attacking his people. Something had to be done, but what? One thing's for sure, he thought, all those muscles on the honcho pig wouldn't stop bullets.

The fruits of Todd Wilm's labors were few (other than Reuben's arrest), but they did serve to put the family on notice that things had changed. No longer was law enforcement willing to deal with gangs as a one crime at a time problem. The gloves were off and the cops weren't going to let anything go untouched, even family. The small amount of dope they found in Borracho's room would not amount to a serious sentence but Erin insisted that the D.A. get a search clause on him because she knew that it would come in handy later. Borracho wasn't going away and the search clause as a condition of his probation would let any peace officer legally search him, his car and his house for three years without probable cause. Defendants usually accepted these search clauses without arguing because they weren't that good at looking into the future and anticipating what problems they may cause them down the road.

His sister had an address book and some phone bills with interesting entries. Some research might pick up a few new gang members' identities and relationships that the department wasn't on to.

Cold Fusion, Intergalactic Travel, and Parenting

Jimmy Scallon called Cam late in the day when he was about ready to go home. He asked him for a meeting and he said it was urgent that it happen today. Every great once and a while Jimmy would call to invite Cam to a social get together or, on rare occasion, to consult him about a law enforcement matter that was unrelated to any active investigations that involved Cam. This urgent thing made this different and Cam was very curious to see what it was all about. They met at Jimmy's residence and, at Jimmy's request, he came alone without telling anyone, even Bobby. It had been gloomy and overcast all day and as Cam pulled up to the concrete and steel ultramodern mansion, he could see the look on Jimmy's face was a good match for the weather. He further assessed it was serious because Jimmy wasn't having his traditional post-work beer.

When Cam got out of his car Jimmy said, "Come in and let me explain the problem. You remember my older brother James, right?"

"Ya, the real estate tycoon."

"Well, he's got a situation that's got to be handled quickly and I'm really not sure where to start."

This was unusual for Jimmy. He was seldom at a loss for how to handle anything. The guy had was an overabundance of confidence.

Jimmy explained, "His oldest daughter Katherine, my godchild, has been giving him trouble. Kat's running around with a rough crowd, drinking, and he's afraid she's doing drugs. What kind he's not sure. There's been some nights she comes home really late, as in the next morning, and is failing everything at school except boys and lunch. We hired a P.I. to see who she's hanging with and where they go but the information doesn't help James fix the current problem.

She's run off and hasn't been back for three days. And the problem is she's hanging around with a bunch of Mexican gang thugs that are into dope, theft, stolen cars and drive-bys. Not to mention prostitution. I know because I've represented a few of them. I'm afraid they'll get her strung out and turn her into a gang prostitute. I have personal knowledge, they've done it before."

Cam had heard this story a dozen times from other citizens but never so close to home.

He responded with, "You do see the irony here, don't you? If you'd have let those pieces of crap go to prison where they belong instead of defending them maybe they wouldn't be out there right now messing with your family." Cam was frequently surprised that seemingly intelligent people couldn't see that their actions had real consequences.

"Cam, I don't need this lecture right now. I need your help." Cam was jolted back from his judgmental mood.

"All right Jimmy, I'm sorry. How old is she now?"

"She's 16."

Cam said, "Well, the official way to proceed is a missing persons report and then we start looking for her if we can develop some probable cause to believe she at a particular location. All this takes time and there are only about eight hundred thousand missing people reported every year in this country."

"Cam, that's exactly why we can't do it by the book. Kat was such a sweet loving little girl. I swear to god, I don't know how she became this jerk. She'll be lost if we wait to do this thing by the numbers, and you and I both know it. It takes forever to go the official route and it almost never saves anyone. There's got to be a way to fix this quickly and quietly and you're the guy who can find it."

Cam leaned back into Jimmy's blue leather sofa directly across from a very large and very expensive nude black-and-white painting and closed his eyes for a minute, pinching the bridge of his nose. He thought about how Jimmy was there for him many years ago when he was a kid and how things would have been different had Jimmy not helped him deal with his crisis that day. He couldn't say no the only time he'd ever really been asked for help. He recalled Kat as a little girl. She was the spitting image of a blond Shirley Temple. She was so outgoing and verbal it was scary coming from such as little kid. He also remembered how spoiled she was, which is probably why this thing had spun out of control like it did. He was thinking that if he did some "off the record" rescue it was the kind of shit that was hard to hide and sure to make a big splash when it happened. He had a history of being a bit wild and what police administrators called a "cowboy," but he'd always understood the limits. This was way beyond the limits of safe conduct. This was like juggling hand grenades.

"All right, Jimmy, who knows about this and what have they done so far."

"Only James and his wife. The P.I. only knows what was in his report. No reports have been made to law enforcement and I know James's wife hasn't told anybody because she's so embarrassed by the whole thing."

"Okay, tell them both not to say anything to anybody till they talk to you. Get me the P.I. report and don't tell anybody I'm involved. I'll start by jacking up a few informants and see if I can help. I'll get back to you in 24 hours."

As Cam drove away he was trying to figure out how to work this thing without telling Bobby. This was likely to require coloring way outside the lines and he really didn't want to get Bobby into trouble if things went south. The good thing was that he had a lot of flexibility in this gang assignment. Cam figured it had to be J-Tra's crew who were involved because his was the only real serious Mexican gang in the local area. The irritating thing was that the two C.I.s that could help with information on this were both Bobby's, but contacting them was a risk he'd have to take. He had to find out where Kat was before he could try to fix things. To add pressure to this mess, Cam was racing the clock. The longer Kat was with these guys the more likely she was to fall into the drug life. Once people start sticking a needle in their arm, the time till addiction sets in is measured on your wrist watch.

Cam figured he would have a few hours to work on finding Kat because Bobby was signed off for the night and he might get most of tomorrow because Bobby was supposed to have court on an old case from when they were on patrol. That might be enough time to get a few things nailed down before he was scheduled to contact Jimmy.

The first thing tonight was to get Ray on this and find out if he knew anything. Cam drove back to the unit office and looked in Bobby's personal snitch file he kept in his lower desk drawer. Most cops don't put everything in the department file because it was subject to leaks. The department tried to follow secure procedure with confidential files, but every once and a while they would do something incredibly stupid like hire a dirt bag's girlfriend as a custodian and give her keys to the whole friggin' department. Bobby's file was hidden within a thick, boring manual on personnel regulations. Cam found numbers for both Ray and Lupe.

Before Cam left the office, he checked his personal email and found the PI report that Jimmy forwarded him. He took a few minutes to read the report, which confirmed Cam's suspicions that J-Tra's boys were involved. Some of the PI's addresses and vehicle registration information confirmed the link.

Ray was a little pissed that Cam wanted to meet in an hour that night but relented when Cam said that this was important and that he had $40 for him for his time.

Cam had to play this close to the vest. He asked about the gang's tactics when they were recruiting new whores without telling him he was specifically interested in an individual person.

Ray said, "I don't know exactly where they take them but from what I've heard it's a house in the city. You got to remember, they usually don't tell me what's going on because they just see me as a kid who wants to hang with them. It's not really like I'm a member of their gang. Only a couple of guys J-Tra calls his pretty boys get to go there and they're the ones that recruited them in the first place and are feeding them the dope. J-Tra figured if everyone knew the location, it would get burned fast so he doesn't tell anybody but the two guys who are working the girls."

Cam got the names of the guys who were working the new girls. In an ideal world, he'd be able to tail them to see if they would lead him to the house. But that would require some help, which he didn't have and couldn't use because he was trying not to let everyone know what he was doing. That tactic would also take time which was slipping away rapidly.

What Cam did notice, though, was that Ray was not loyal to the gang anymore and really wanted to be far away from them.

His hope was that Lupe might be able to help identify the house where she had been force-fed drugs and if the location hadn't changed since she was held there. All this questioning of informants was bound to get back to Bobby but Cam had few options because he was playing against the clock and if he was going to get this done before they had Kat completely strung out and addicted he had to cut corners and move fast. If he asked the CI's not to tell Bobby, that was the fastest way to make sure they did. Safety was a victim of speed in situations like this and there really wasn't any way around it.

Lupe was a little help but she wasn't committed like Ray and it was Bobby that she really trusted. She started off saying, "I don't know what you're talking about," but then softened when Cam started to tell her about how the parents were worried sick and how Kat's mom won't eat or sleep. It was giving out too much information but Cam had no choice but to risk it. She eventually said there was a house on the west side between 4th and 19th somewhere north of South Julian Street that the gang owned. She added that she wasn't recruited that way so any information she had, came second hand from other girls. The clue she gave that might break something loose was that the house was occupied by a crankster couple.

She said, "They keep their mouths shut because they get free housing. The place has a studio apartment in the alley that they live in and they take care of the front house and feed the girls. Sometimes they stay in the front when J-Tra's guys want to leave."

All Cam had to do was find a meth addict that gave that general area as their residence upon booking and he might catch a break. It was a given that anybody on crank would get busted regularly because they were so driven to get money that they would eventually run afoul of the law. What he really needed was help from records division. One of the girls that worked there could do this search for him in no time, but once again he was letting more people in on this than he should. A secret is only a secret if you don't tell anybody and he was giving way too many pieces of information out.

Jane Nevins was a records clerk he dated for several months about a half year ago. He really liked her but she made it clear she wanted a serious relationship because her biological clock was ticking and she wanted a family. He ran away because that's not what he wanted. Maybe it was time to see how pissed she was, because he really needed some help. He walked over to records and stopped in front of Jane's desk. She looked up and didn't hide her surprise very well.

She said, "Cam, thought you died."

"No, Jane but I'm close. Could we talk in private?"

She stared at him for a few seconds trying to access what this was all about and then said, "The break room in 5 minutes." As she wondered about the possible motivations for this encounter, she reminded herself that Cam was as difficult as he was attractive. She also reminded herself that she was still angry with him.

As Cam sat at a far table from the door sipping his coffee he saw her walking toward him. She carried herself like an athlete because she ran and lifted weights, but the thing that Cam really noticed was that she walked like she was naked. The way her feet searched the ground for a next step, the way she moved her arms was erotic as hell. Maybe he was just picturing how she used to look when she got out of his shower and walked into his unfinished kitchen for something to eat or how she bent over to rub Nick's head as she walked by him. He wondered if everybody else noticed this or if it was just him. As he watched other men watching her he decided that most guys noticed her but their interest wasn't as obsessive as his. Any 5'11" beautiful woman was bound to attract a few eyes but she actually made him lose his concentration momentarily. He had trouble trying to remember why he walked away from her and was asking himself if he'd screwed up. The thought of someone else with her made him jealous and that made no sense at all. No wonder he was having dreams about her.

As she sat down with a smile on her face she said, "All right, Mr. Independent. What brings you to my world?"

Cam explained only that he had an emergency and was trying to find a house. He also said, "I need it to be off the record."

She stared at him for a minute and said, "I hope this isn't something that will bite me later on."

Cam told her, "If someone asks you could lay it back on me and say that the request came in over the phone and that it was an emergency. That you were told the official paper request would be in soon."

She nodded and said, "All right. I'll see what I can do."

Cam gave her a cell number he had just acquired and told her to make the call from another clerk's phone.

"It's not that I'm paranoid but you never know." Cam did know that everything you did could be traced: phone calls, net searches, record checks, the works. Nothing can be accessed without leaving a track. The only way to get around it was to use someone who wasn't a suspect or access a data bank that no one was watching. The day of looking in a paper file and getting information was over.

It took Jane about three hours to call him. She said, "I found several houses with an A and B address meaning there were two houses on one lot in the area you identified. Only one had a corresponding arrest for meth. I hand wrote all the information and put it in your mail box. Hope it helps."

"Jane, I really appreciate this. Is it okay if I call you?"

Jane said, "Sure, Hero. I'll just go home and hold my breath," then she hung up.

Cam had to admit, he had that coming. His behavior had been pretty bad but he could deal with all that later. The clock was running and he had to get Kat out of that house if she was there.

What Cam needed now was a cool car. One that didn't attract attention or come back registered to him if shit went bad. He owned an old F150 truck. It was a hunk of junk he bought off a guy who had wrecked it not far from Cam's house. When Cam had heard the crash, he jogged down to see what happened. He found a pissed off guy with a crunched fender and a flat tire with his truck in a ditch up against an oak tree. Cam offered him three hundred dollars on the spot and the guy sold it and phoned for a ride. Cam never switched the registration because he was working on it and not really driving it on the roads. He'd replaced the fender and tire but the whole thing needed a paint job and a few extras. Cam liked the 4-wheel drive for getting work done on the property and the price was right. He would use it to check out the house and if the plates were run by some officer, the old owner really didn't know who he sold it to since Cam had picked up the registration later at the owner's house. The lack of current tabs was a problem, but he would just have to hope a little smear of mud on the rear plate and dropping the tail gate to block the view of the plate would get him through. He grabbed the .45 automatic he'd liberated from the gangster thug and since he'd already test fired it on the back of his property he felt confident it would be enough fire power if things got ugly. He didn't want to use his Glock because they're test fired at the factory and had ballistic records on file that can be matched to a slug or shell casing. Cam had an assortment of holsters he had acquired through the years and one was perfect for a .45 autoloader.

He parked on the street about half a block away from the gang safe house that Jane had found for him and settled in for a long stake out because this could take a while. It wouldn't be smart to rush the place in the day and he needed to be sure about this information because it was so sketchy. After several hours, a woman in her mid-forties driving a SUV pulled into the driveway with two kids in tow. Cam knew instantly that she wasn't right for this place.

Something was wrong, "Shit!"

Cam slowly went by and snagged the plate on the SUV. Then he drove to an internet café about six blocks away. First, he ran the plate through DMV and got the registered owner's name. Then he Googled up the address and found there was a real estate listing for the place indicating that it was just sold. This was a huge setback. He'd lost another day and Kat was no closer to being located. If he couldn't find the right house and find it soon she could possibly be moved out of town and would probably be so strung out there would be no chance of salvaging her.

He needed to think and he was exhausted. Things were not coming to him the way they normally did. His confidence was shaky and every solution he'd come up with was crap. So, he went home and decided he and the pooch would go for a run and eat something. He also needed sleep. Maybe that would awaken some dormant ideas. When he got back from his run he called Jimmy on his new cell and told him what was up. Jimmy had the same sense of desperation that Cam did. He feared the ever-ticking clock. Cam told him he'd come up with something and call him back. He had a beer, half of a baked chicken and broccoli before he fell asleep.

When he awoke from a short rest he stepped out his front door and watched the night lights of the city in the distance as he scratched Nick's neck.

"Hope I don't get caught doing this crazy shit, partner, or you'll have to live in the city for a while."

As Cam and Nick sat on the porch, he suddenly became aware that he was at one of those crossroads in life where the decisions he'd make would likely alter his personal trajectory forever. So often we just go along day to day and knock down problems and try to move forward on goals we set months and years ago without ever rethinking where we're headed. Situations like the one he was in now caused a person to stop and look at the big picture.

His dad was a sailor before he got married and had a family. He liked to tell the kids that were old enough to understand, "You have to box your compass every once and a while." It was a term used by pre-GPS navigators when they'd set sail across the ocean which came from the practice of sailing back and forth between two fixed geographic points and making sure your compass was set accurately. What he meant to convey to the kids was that they needed to look at their life periodically and make sure the goals and direction they had set for themselves were still accurate. The hard truth was that, as we age and mature, our goals change, and pursuing outdated life goals will ultimately prove very unsatisfying. This bit of craziness Cam was involved in now caused him to box his compass on several of his life decisions like his love life, career goals and personal values. Most of all it caused him to examine if he could live with himself if he did the safe thing, which was nothing. Not being a man who was given to analysis paralysis, he made up his mind.

Cam knew what he had to do but recognized it was dangerous and he'd have to be lucky. Very lucky. But then, he usually was.

He gathered up a few pieces of equipment he would need in a canvas bag and threw it behind the seat of his truck. He then drove back to the city to find one of the two guys Ray had identified as the pretty boys who recruited the young girls. Either one of them would know where Kat was, and it was time to make shit happen. He set up on the gang house on 14th since it was late and he'd figured it was the most likely place to find one of them. He'd run them earlier and had two sets of vehicle descriptions that belonged to the two pretty boys. The problem was that there was nothing that said they'd be in their own cars. It was just a chance he'd have to take. He settled in for a long code 5. This wasn't the best idea he'd ever had but it was the only thing he could come up with so it would have to do. He had to find out where Kat was fast and there were no other options.

Cam was having a hard time staying awake because nothing was happening at the house and he had the heater on due to a chilly evening. While he listened to the department radio dispatches on a portable radio he had snagged, to make sure he wasn't targeted as a suspicious person, he played multiple scenarios in his head trying to figure what options he would have if this thing went down in different ways. Some of the outcomes were just plain bad so he would have to try and make things go down the right way. He thought about competitive divers mentally going through their dive rotations and twists to get the desired outcome and was convinced if he planned this well he could make a splash-less entry also.

At about four hours into the stake-out, a lowered, white Honda drove up to the house. It was on his list of cars owned by one of the two pretty boys. This one belonged to Pedro Garcia, a skinny twenty-three-year-old who had been busted for beating the crap out of a reported girlfriend two years earlier and possession of meth six months later. The victim of the beating was probably another girl they recruited to work the streets. The driver, if it was Pedro, let a guy out at the house and kept on driving. Cam pulled his truck in behind the Honda as it pulled away and from the looks of his route, he was headed home across town. Cam kept his distance so as to not burn the surveillance. He had trouble finding other cars to hide behind due to the late hour. The problem Cam was contemplating was how to get Pedro out of the car and into custody without anyone noticing and parking his car in an out of the way place. As Cam followed him he started to hatch an idea.

When they were in a quiet part of town with very little traffic that late in the evening, Cam pulled up behind Pedro at a stop sign. He slowed but didn't stop and ran into the back of Pedro's car. It wasn't a fender crunching hit, but it was enough to make damage a real possibility.

Cam backed up a couple of feet and yelled out the window, "Pull over to a parking lot and we'll see what damage was done." It worked. Pedro followed him to the adjacent parking lot and got out of the car mad as hell. He was strutting and waving his arms.

"What the fuck is the matter with you Ese? You drive like a fucking –"

Cam greeted him with a .45 between his eyes so close he almost hit him with the barrel. "Police, you're under arrest. Get down on your knees."

As Pedro slowly dropped to his knees Cam holstered his weapon and cuffed Pedro. He pushed him on his face and cuffed a pair of transportation chains on his ankles. He stood Pedro up and had him shuffle over to the passenger door of the truck but before he loaded him he pulled out a dog leash that he used when he walked Nick in the city. He snapped the leash onto the hand cuff chain, ran it under the leg iron chain, and pulled it back over the cuff chain again. As he pulled it tighter and tighter Pedro was bent back till his head was in danger of touching his heels. Cam shoved him face down on the truck seat and tied off the leash to the crook's ankle chain.

At this point, Pedro figured out that this wasn't a normal arrest. This cop was in a truck and was hog-tying him like a rodeo cowboy ties a steer. Something wasn't right. As he started to protest Cam shut the door and walked over to Pedro's Honda. He drove it a short distance between two parked commuter cars and locked it up. When he got back to the truck Pedro was asking questions, yelling and threatening Cam with everything from lawsuits to death. Fortunately, no one was around to hear him.

Cam figured he'd better get their relationship off to a correct start so he pulled Pedro's head up by a hand full of hair and slapped him as hard as he could across the face.

He said, "Shut the fuck up and maybe I won't kill you." Then, he threw Pedro on the floor of his truck where he lay quietly.

Pedro was scared. This was not right at all. Something was very, very wrong.

Cam drove out toward the city limits. He knew of a park that was under renovation where he could talk to Pedro without being disturbed. When he got to the dirt road with barricades Cam got out and moved the one that wasn't locked down and drove through. He'd been here several times back when he was on patrol. He then replaced the metal post and drove on. After about a mile and a half he pulled over to the side of the road following a dirt road behind a grove of trees where he got out of the truck. Alum Rock Park was dark with only a little moon light that night but it was light enough to see Pedro's face and he could see that Pedro was terrified. He hauled him out of the truck and threw him down on the dry grass. Cam looked up at the night sky and thought if it weren't for dealing with this crazy chain of events he'd be home taking Nick for a walk in the cool evening breeze.

The truck's dome light from the open passenger door gave Cam just enough light to see what he wanted. He loosened the leash a little so Pedro could straighten out somewhat even though his legs were still tucked under him.

Cam said, "Comfy, Pedro? I'm going to ask you some questions and you're going to tell me the truth and if you're a good little boy you just might get to go home tonight. But if you lie to me, I'm going to hurt you so bad you'll wish you were dead. Now, let's get started. I know you and your buddy Juan have been doping two school girls to make them street whores for the gang. I need to know where they are, right now."

Pedro scared and angry, said, "You must be crazy. I don't know what you're talking about, man. If you don't let me go my boys will kill you and your whole fucking family. You fucked up big time. You hear me, Cabron?"

Cam smiled at him and said, "Some people have to learn things the hard way." He got into the truck and pulled out a canvas beach bag with tools in it. As he sat on Pedro's stomach he took a nylon tie down strap and wrapped it around Pedro's head several times and ran one loop across his mouth forcing it open. He tied it off tight so he could control Pedro's head by the strap. Pedro fought and tried to resist but with the cuffs and leg irons being tied together and Cam sitting on him he could do nothing but swear. Cam took out a can of keyboard cleaner that he had purchased several weeks ago.

He replaced the long plastic spray tube with half of a plastic Q-tip that had a hollow center running the length of it. The Q-tip would hold the freezing liquid together as it gathered around the cotton tip.

He asked Pedro, "Have you ever had a tooth tested at the dentists to see if it was alive? Guess not. Well you're going to love this. First let me read you the warning label. *Liquid contents may cause frostbite on contact with skin. Contact physician if such contact occurs.* You just tell old Doctor Cop here if it hurts, okay, Shithead?" Cam held the strap on the side of Pedro head in a firm grip, inverted the can and sprayed the freezing cold compressed propellant as he held the cotton tip against one of Pedro's badly decayed molars. You can always count on meth users to have a set of teeth that look like rotten corn. As Cam held the Q-tip against his tooth it only took three seconds before Pedro was screaming out of a muffled tie down strap and begging Cam to stop.

Cam said, "Where are they and don't lie to me because I already have some information. If you lie I'll know. And I promise I'll finish this can and use the second can in this bag till all your teeth look like icicles on a cabin roof."

Pedro said, in a muffled lisp, "I'm not sure, man, and they'll kill me if I tell you anything."

Cam just nodded, "Okay Pedro I see where you're coming from" and then he pulled the trigger again and held it down for a good 10 seconds. Pedro was screaming, bucking and trying to get away but Cam was sitting on his chest and just kept spraying. Pedro's bladder released and he pissed his pants. He was a full-blown mess by the time Cam stopped. It took a couple of minutes before the freezing subsided and he could calm down and breathe well enough to talk.

Through tears, snot, twitching face muscles, and nausea Pedro said, "They moved them out of the city. It was getting too hot for them and neighbors started asking questions so they took them to Mountain View. The Nuestra Familia has a house there. I don't know exactly where it is because J-Tra has some of the other guys feeding the girls their dope."

Cam smiled at Pedro and said, "You know, Pedro, some people are just slow learners and need remedial education."

Cam produced a small hammer from his bag and grabbed Pedro's upper lip in his left hand. He peeled it back toward his nose then he then gave a quick sharp smack to his front teeth with the hammer. One of the teeth broke off with a diagonal crack that ran up to the gum line.

As Pedro was screaming, Cam inverted the can and said, "The other guys aren't allowed around the girls. Just the two of you pretty boys. And you've been to the house several times because escrow closed on the old house two weeks ago." Then Cam sprayed the broken tooth with a long cold shot.

Pedro started screaming "South El Monte, 1607 in Mountain View, 1607 South El Monte."

This sounded like Pedro was finally telling the truth. Cam remembered a gang investigator's meeting where police agencies shared information on their local gangs with one another. One of the investigators from Mountain View mentioned a house on South El Monte that was owned by the Nuestra Familia that they thought was weird because it had almost no traffic coming or going out of it. They thought at the time it might be for one of the gang members' parents but now Cam had a different thought.

Cam proceeded to ask Pedro a dozen other questions about the gang operation. He knew the answers to most of the questions and was only checking to see if Pedro was still comfortable with a lie. He would ask an occasional question about the girls like what drug they were using on them and Cam felt like the answers were truthful. Apparently, Pedro didn't want the frozen tooth experience again.

Cam stood up and looked at Pedro who was crying like a baby and said, "You know Pedro, I believe you and just to reward you for your honesty I'll going to let you go. Do you see this tape recorder in my pocket?"

Cam held his jacket open so Pedro could see the recorder and Pedro nodded. Cam said, "I'm not even going to share it with J-Tra if you're a good boy. That way you won't get killed by the big boys for being a rat. That sound like a good idea?" Pedro just nodded through his occasional sobs.

Cam said, "When you get that tooth capped I'd get one of those big gold ones. Those are totally cool, chicks really dig those." Cam could see that Pedro was already thinking of that possibility as something he could warm to.

Cam looked down at Pedro and said in a deep, serious voice, "Pedro, the only ones that know what happened here tonight are you and me. If you open your mouth, your people will kill you for talking. You understand?" Pedro nodded because he knew it was true. He was safe as long as he told no one.

Cam also told him, "You are one lucky asshole because if I turn in the tape you would be jailed for 100 fucking years for kidnapping, rape, and drugging people and pimping. All with a prior record and gang penalty added to your sentence." He told him he'd never get out of prison and the only sex he'd ever have is being bent over the end of a prison bed in the middle of the night. Cam threw all his tools in the bag and put it in the truck. He unlocked Pedro's cuffs, gave him his car keys and told him to start walking. He figured that even if Pedro was stupid enough to tell anybody, which he doubted, he'd still have to walk out of the park and back to civilization before he could phone anybody because Cam took his cell phone. That would give Cam enough time to get Kat out of the house. He never told Pedro that there was no tape in the recorder. The last thing he needed was evidence of his torture session. He wasn't a complete fool and he always remembered the lessons of the Nixon administration. Don't record yourself doing crime.

Letting a serious criminal like Pedro walk was hard to swallow. But everything Cam did was illegal as hell and he knew that no court in the land would let the evidence in, so he had no alternative but to let him go. The feeling Cam had as Pedro walked away was similar to the day OJ was found not guilty of murder. In the pit of his stomach there was a sick moment where the world was not right.

Now the second part of the plan, the most important part, was getting Kat free. There were several ways it could play out. He could notify law enforcement anonymously that there were two captive girls in the house on South El Monte Street, but that tactic had its drawbacks because if they were slow or didn't believe the call was for real, a rescue could get botched. And there was always the problem of where Cam got his information. Official tactics like search warrants took a lot of time and with Pedro free that was dangerous. The gang might get them moved before they could be rescued, or, worse yet, might silence them permanently. It might also draw heat to him because all calls are recorded and even disguised voices were a piece of evidence. Not notifying law enforcement just might keep him off the radar.

Cam decided that the best way to get this thing done was to do it himself in a blitz style raid. Security at the house where the girls were stashed couldn't be too serious because it would draw attention and two whores in training weren't worth that much effort by J-Tra's people. It would really be nice to have Bobby along and do what they did so many times together, but he couldn't do that to him. This is the kind of stuff that ends careers and earns cops jail time if they're caught.

Cam caught the 101 freeway and headed toward Mountain View. His adrenaline was pumping and his stomach had that feeling he always got before a final karate match at a competition. On the way to the house he drove around the back of a grocery store and threw the bag of tools in a dumpster. If things did turn to shit he needed to keep evidence that could be used against him to a minimum. As he arrived at the hostage house the sun was just starting to rise. His fatigue was temporarily abated by the adrenaline now pumping through his body. He drove down the street twice and couldn't see anything unusual so he parked his truck about 100 yards beyond the address and did his best to hide his face. He pulled up his collar and buttoned the foul weather button that held the collar around his cheeks. He put on a ball cap and big dark glasses. The coat covered the front of his face so his mouth and chin didn't show and he guessed he didn't look too much like a 211 stick-up man unless you looked at him straight on. He sat in the truck and watched the neighborhood for a few minutes looking for signs of life. Normally this tactical assessment of the area and people's activities would have lasted a lot longer to really get the lay of the land and all the dangers present, but this was early morning and waiting would only result in more people waking up. He decided to go for it, but before he did he grabbed one more piece of equipment he had in his inside jacket pocket.

Several years ago, an uncle of his came through town for a short overnight visit and forgot his hearing aids.

When Cam called him, and asked if he needed Cam to mail them to him the uncle told him "No, they're an old pair that don't have all the new technology features on them so I don't want them."

He added, "Cam, you might want to put one of them on when you want to listen-in on people because you can turn them up to magnify sound, way beyond the normal hearing range. That could give a guy in your profession a real edge." Cam tried it a couple of times and was blown away by how well and how far away you could pick up conversations. After he had it plugged into his left ear he decided the time was now, so he walked up to the front door of this 1960's flat top stucco house and quietly tested the knob. When he found that it was locked, he went around to the rear. He was hoping the cranksters that were watching the place were their usually sloppy selves and left something open. The back door was locked also, but houses from this era often had a window in the door. This one did with screen covering it and it was open slightly. Cam took out his knife, locked the blade and quietly slit the screen. He reached in and unlocked the door. As he walked silently across the filthy kitchen with his hand on his holstered gun and up the hall, he found a door with an outside bolt lock. This had to be where the girls were. If he was lucky he might just sneak in grab Kat and sneak out without anybody knowing, but that was asking for a lot of luck. For a split second, he stopped and listened with his bionic ear for any movement inside the house. Hearing nothing but some snoring and the refrigerator motor he slid the bolt quietly and eased the door open. This hearing device was not only helping him hear the slightest sound but it was helping him be extra quiet because his own movements and sounds were exaggerated.

When he stepped inside the bolted door it took a few seconds before his eyes adjusted to the dark conditions of the room because plywood had been nailed over the windows. He saw two girls handcuffed to two single beds wearing nothing but their underwear bottoms. They saw him when he entered but were too doped up to figure out what was happening so they just lay there staring. He put his finger to his lips and motioned for them to stay where they were. He recognized Kat and it didn't appear as though she recognized him because of his disguise. Or maybe she was just too doped up to notice. He took out his cuff key and undid Kat's cuff in the metal bed headboard so it didn't clank around. As he was un-cuffing her wrist he heard a very faint noise with the help of his bionic ear piece, coming from down the hall. He motioned to Kat to lie down again, put the cuffs in his back pocket and threw the sheet over her wrist. He then went back by the door and hid behind it.

A skinny tweaking 30-year-old crankster stepped into the room wearing nothing but a pair of boxer shorts and a dirty tank top carrying a nasty looking homemade Billy club in his hand. He started to ask, "What the fuck is going......" when Cam delivered a closed fist karate punch to the back of his head right behind the ear that was so hard it knocked him out cold. As he folded in two Cam pulled the crook's t-shirt over his head from the back which was an old cop trick to stop suspects from spitting on officers. The result was that the crankster couldn't see anything and Cam cuffed him up behind his back with the cuffs he pulled off of Kat. He then threw him in a closet and shoved a heavy dresser in front of the door. He stood Kat up and put a sheet around her shoulders and told her to hold it in front.

Kat was wobbly on her feet but looked at the other girl and said, "Take her too." Cam nodded and un-cuffed the other girl. As he pulled her wrist out to uncuff it he noticed that the girl had smuggled a piece of glass from somewhere and slit her wrist several times very deeply. There was a large puddle of blood that had soaked into the sheets and mattress. Cam shuddered because this girl had no color to her skin and looked close to dying. She was so out of it that it took both Kat and Cam to get her up and help her out the front door. About half way there, Cam decided it would be easier to carry her, since no one else was between the truck and them. He threw her over his left shoulder leaving his gun hand free. Apparently, Mrs. Crankster could sleep through anything because they made it out of the house without a problem.

Cam loaded both of them in the truck and drove to a nearby hospital. It wasn't the smartest tactical move but the other girl was so low on blood that she wasn't even bleeding anymore and she looked like she could die without immediate treatment.

On the way Cam called Jimmy with his cold cell and said, "I've got Kat and another girl and I'm in route to the hospital. Tell your brother not to talk over the phone but get over here."

The thought crossed Cam's mind that, "You can really get a lot done quickly when you don't follow any rules."

Jimmy was the first one there and met Cam in the parking lot. Cam explained to him that he had already snagged a wheelchair that was located by the front door of the E.R. for the other girl.

He had told Kat, who could barely walk, "Push the wheelchair through the double doors and tell the intake nurse that you and the other girl have been given street drugs against your will and the other girl has lost a lot of blood."

As he talked with Jimmy in the back parking lot and told him, "I'm afraid camera surveillance might have spotted me in the entrance getting the wheelchair," he started to realize what he had done.

Jimmy could tell Cam was worried and just smiled, "Time to get rid of that truck and all those clothes. Ambrose will be in touch with you. Cam, I love you buddy," as he gave him a hug that was embarrassingly long.

As Cam drove home exhausted he thought, "What the fuck have I done, besides committed kidnap, robbery (the punk's cell phone), torture, mayhem, burglary, felony assault, civil rights violations under the color of law and no telling what other felonies a D.A. might come up with. This could get me like a thousand damn years in jail. But, what I guess I have done is saved two young girls from a life of drug addiction, beatings, and prostitution and that's not a bad day's work."

He also thought about torture as a tool to fight evil. A nation can't sanction it or they become as bad as the enemy they're fighting, but everyone can justify it on a personal level when it's used to save someone they love. He'd add this brain twister to the rest of the moral conflicts he was continually working on when the lights went out.

He went to bed that night with his mind spinning.

DAMAGE CONTROL

The next morning Cam reached out from a tangled bed sheet and answered his phone to a voice that boomed, "Open your fucking eyes and treat this day as if it was one more adventure in paradise!"

"Good morning, Ambrose."

"We'll see about that. Where and when can we meet?"

Cam thought a moment, "I'll be in a café on 19th Street just north of Taylor about 11:00 a.m. today. Could you meet me there?"

"Done." Ambrose hung up.

Cam's meeting spot with Ambrose had a dual purpose. He was almost certain he needed a good attorney, and he also needed a ride home since he planned to sell his truck at the San Jose flea market five blocks away from the café, to the first guy with cash. He had been assigned there a couple of times to look for stolen property and illegal gun sales. It was a freewheeling "kasbah" where you could unload anything if you knew who to talk with. Cam had already put all of the clothes he wore the night of Pedro's interview in a trash bin, so outside of the cell phone which he'd ditch soon, he hadn't left any physical evidence that he could think of. He did clean the cuffs and leg irons and keep them because they were department property. The .45 and a few other toys were kept in a place that was next to impossible to find and would require a dog that could smell underwater to locate it. Thank the stars for his kayaking dry bags.

Ambrose started their meeting in a quiet back booth by saying, "Cam, I don't want you to say shit for a couple of minutes. I need to explain something to you and I need your undivided attention." Cam nodded and waited.

"First, cops make shitty clients. They have just enough knowledge to make them think they know something when they don't. You know how to make a case but you don't know how to make a case go away. That's my job and I'm good at it. So, you're going to have to get used to following orders.

Second, I don't want to know anything you did because there may come a time, if we're unlucky, where you have to take the witness stand. If you tell me something went down in a specific way I can't introduce you to testify to something different if I know its perjury. They call that Suborning Perjury and attorneys get jailed and disbarred for that. So, we'll keep it general and try to guide you into a good position to deal with any fallout. You, of course, have attorney / client privilege so anything you tell me is protected unless you plan on killing someone."

Cam just nodded and said, "I appreciate your help, Ambrose, and I hope it all blows over but we both know that that's a long shot."

Ambrose said, "Okay, who knows anything about this and how much?"

Cam thought a minute and said, "A punk named Pedro but he has a lot of incentive to stay quiet."

"Is he 'damaged' in any way?"

"A broken tooth, but that's minor."

Ambrose said, "Okay, who else?"

"Jimmy and his brother, but neither of them knows any details."

"My partner will pick up something I'm sure, but I told him zero and will get him to let it go."

"There's a female records clerk that did some record checks for me but I didn't explain anything and she used secure communications."

"I also asked two CI's for any information about the house but they won't give up anything for fear of gang revenge."

"There was a guy at the house but he never saw my face and he won't talk with law enforcement anyway because he'd have to admit to kidnapping and false imprisonment."

"The biggie is the two girls. I have no idea how much they said or if they could recognize me or not and I know they are going to be interviewed as soon as possible.

So, I think the trail is pretty cold except for the damn video from the hospital. I was still wearing my big coat with the collar up, hat and dark glasses so I don't think it's a good picture."

Ambrose said, "I'm assuming you no longer have those items of clothing."

"Correct. They're gone."

"Are the CI's in official files?"

"No."

"Good, keep it that way."

Ambrose made a note to talk with Jimmy and make sure his brother was admonished to keep quiet. He was almost certain Jimmy had enough forethought to speak to the two girls but he'd check that also. He sure hoped that Jimmy handled that the night of the incident because that would be the first thing Mountain View cops would check.

Ambrose told Cam that if he were questioned about this by anybody in his agency or Mountain View police that he should invoke "Miranda" and request an attorney be present.

He also said, "Forget Lybarger." The case said cops can be ordered under threat of discipline to cooperate with an IA investigation and not lose Miranda rights on the criminal charges. Years ago, officers were ordered to explain a shooting or other act under threat of termination for insubordination if they didn't. The courts came back with a decision that said they could be ordered to talk but that the statements couldn't be used in a criminal prosecution. "This is not something you can discuss. Deny everything even if it means getting fired. The facts would get you fired anyway. We'll deal with that separately."

As Cam sat there trying to think what he should ask Ambrose, Ambrose looked across the table and smiled.

He said, "Cam, I deal with shit like this all the time. You need to act like nothing out of the ordinary has happened. It will be difficult for you but our plan is to wait and see what comes our way. This is not a situation where we can go out and start asking questions. Your job is to be your old typical outrageous, irreverent self. Bust bad guys and torture those you love with your never-ending sarcasm and irreverence. Any change in your behavior will make people suspicious. Got it?" Cam nodded. "The ball is in my court. Let me handle it. I'll tell you if I need something done. You can take some comfort in the fact that juries seldom punish heroes for saving two young girls from gang rapists."

As Ambrose slid his considerable person out of the booth he said, "Now, pay the bill and where can I drop you?"

While Cam was riding with Ambrose back to his house to pick up his car he got a call from Bobby.

"Hey Wild Man, where the heck have you been? You blew off three of my calls and it hasn't been easy covering for you."

"I know, Bobby, I'll explain it as soon as I get in. I need to do a couple of things and I'll be at the department in about two hours."

"Okay, Cam, we'll talk then."

Ambrose looked over at Cam and said, "Don't explain too much. Anybody can get served with a subpoena." Cam nodded.

As Cam drove into work he tried to think about anything he'd missed but he had to let some of the stuff go and hope Ambrose and Jimmy would cover it. Ambrose would soon be informed by Jimmy that he had already talked with the two girls and was in fact representing them under the guise of concern over potential criminal charges for drug usage. Jimmy was his old masterful self when he approached the two girls. He explained that his legal representation would be for free because he was related to Kat and that since they were involved with the gang together their case was intertwined so that they could damage each other if their testimony wasn't coordinated. He suggested that any admissions or statements could cause them problems with law enforcement so they should limit their comments to: "I don't remember because I was too incapacitated and I can't identify any one." He told them to invoke "Miranda" and refuse to talk beyond that initial statement unless their attorney was present. Kat seem to understand the purpose for Uncle Jimmy's tactics as she just smiled and nodded when he told them it was the safest thing to do for everybody. The other girl and her parents were just grateful to have such a high-powered attorney at their disposal. He went into great detail about how law enforcement would promise them that they weren't the target here but that they were only after the gang. He explained that the cops would even guarantee them immunity in writing but that all that was a trick they often used, so the girls had to rely on him because he was family and the only one who had their best interests at heart.

Jimmy felt that he had thrown up a solid brick wall where the girls and his brother were concerned. He knew the cops would be pissed but that was nothing new in his business. Just wait till they found out the girls were scheduled to go to a rehabilitation hospital out of state for a three-month stay, courtesy of Kat's well-to-do father.

∞

As Cam entered the squad room Sgt. Glen walked up to him and said, "I hope you're feeling better because we've got lots of work backing up here. What was wrong with you anyway?" Cam was at a loss for an answer when he saw Bobby behind the Sergeant, in the other corner of the squad room. Bobby was motioning with his finger down his throat and Cam said," I guess it was just a case of the flu because I couldn't keep anything down." The Sergeant looked at him for a few seconds, nodded and walked off.

As they both sat down at their desks and began to go through their mail and other briefing sheets, Cam said, "Thanks, Bobby."

Bobby said, "You'll have to explain this to me sometime."

Cam said, "As much as I can." Cam then rolled his chair over to Bobby's desk, opened his lower desk drawer and pulled out his CI file. He handed it to Bobby and said, "I think it would be safer for you to keep these at home from now on."

Bobby just looked puzzled and said, "Right," as he slid the file into his leather case.

Bobby didn't like this secret crap. Partners were supposed to trust each other, but then Cam normally did. This must be some bad stuff if Cam wouldn't share what he'd been up to. That meant that it was a lot worse than his normal wild-ass behavior. If Cam didn't at least attempt to satisfy his curiosity about the last few days he just might have to nibble around the edges of this and see what he could find out.

Bobby had forgotten that he had some news for Cam and he wasn't sure he wanted to share it with him in the middle of all the resent chaos, but he figured Cam would find out with or without Bobby's help.

"Hey Cam, while you were AWOL, a couple of homicide detectives contacted me about a business card they found in the victim's purse on a case they got over the weekend. A prostitute was found in a park restroom ODed on heroin. The body was discovered early in the morning by a citizen and the autopsy will probably show death was from a massive dose of heroin because an outfit they found next to the body tested positive for high purity dope. It looks like it could be a homicide because the victim doesn't have injection sites that show IV drug use in her arms other than the one that killed her. She was always very careful to fix in areas that didn't show. Dawn Robinson had your card stuffed under her driver's license. Who'd have thought she would have kept it? Looks like they thought she was the snitch in their organization. I told detectives what we knew but they didn't think they had much to work with so I guess that's just one more body we'll have to chalk up to J-Tra."

Cam stood up and walked in silence toward the locker room, his guilt, frustration and rage barely under control. He gave the squad room bulletin board an elbow smash that left a two-inch dent as he exited the room. Everyone was quietly watching Cam, then Bobby as he just waited a few minutes before he joined Cam.

Sergeant Glen was not a fool. He'd been listening to people lie to him for thirty god damn years and cops were no better at it than anybody else. In fact, they were worse because they felt bad about lying, usually. He wasn't sure what was going on with Cam and Bobby, but whatever it was probably wasn't too extreme because Bobby was a part of it and he was so squeaky clean it hurt. His best guess was a personal issue like a broken heart or a drunken lost weekend. He'd watch it for a while and hope it was nothing that affected the police department. He had plenty to do without getting involved in these boneheads' personal lives.

Ambrose on the other hand wanted to get involved, but he'd done most of the damage control he could without causing neon signs to start flashing over Cam's head. The biggie here was the video. He could hope for a sloppy Mountain View cop who just overlooked asking for it but that was asking for a little too much. He had met most of their investigators and they were pretty thorough. Maybe it would just be a bad picture and they could all go back to their normal lives. He'd keep his ear to the ground on this one and see if any of the administration was paying attention to the recent events surrounding the rescue. He had several sources on the MV police department: one female cop who was fighting through an ugly divorce and custody dispute, another cop who was being disciplined over an off-duty drinking incident and his best source was a Sergeant who worked off the books, doing investigations for the law firm.

WAITING FOR THE CALL

Cam wasn't good at waiting. His whole life he had been the kind of guy who hit thing head on, but this wasn't one of those situations. The only tactic that would work was to sit back and see if anything happened. It was a lot like waiting to see if your cancer lab test returned positive. To make it worse he couldn't even pretend to care because that would draw attention to him.

So, he decided to take Ambrose's advice and do his job like he had before the rescue, balls to the wall. Now he had even more incentive to jail that piece of shit J-Tra. He didn't fool himself into thinking he'd stopped the gang from ruining young girls' lives. He only helped two girls. Many more would follow if he couldn't jail this asshole.

As he and Bobby got into the Mustang the next day, Bobby said, "Okay Hero, you want to tell what's been going on?"

Cam shook his head slightly and said, "Bobby, this crap will get all over anybody who touches it. I'm doing you a huge favor by leaving you out of it. Please leave it at that." Bobby nodded and started to drive them out of the parking lot, but he wasn't about to let it drop. Nothing gets a cop's interest like telling him not to be interested.

Bobby told Cam, "We have to be back at the P.D. by 11:00 a.m. for a search warrant briefing. The narcs have a buy bust going down and will be serving a warrant at two different sites after lunch. They needed a lot of manpower so they tapped the gang unit and a few patrol officers to cover everything they need to do."

Cam asked Bobby, "What's the plan was for the next hour?"

Bobby told him, "Let's check out a few houses and talk with some C.I.s until briefing time."

Cam hoped that Ray and Lupe wouldn't talk about his contacting them if they were the informants Bobby had planned to talk to. This was just one more example of how this rescue slopped over into other things. He guessed he'd just minimize the contact and ask Bobby to let it go if it got brought up.

Bobby and Cam couldn't find any of their informants and all the gang hangouts appeared unusually quiet. Cam couldn't help but wonder if everybody was lying low because he'd kicked over the proverbial hornets' nest. When incidents like this occurred in gang country everybody was waiting for the other shoe to drop. Paranoid criminals just knew the cops were going to raid them any minute. There was also the fear of an inside informant. Crooks were suspicious of each other and paranoid that someone would think they were the snitch. The slightest rumor could cause a chain reaction that could mean serious grief for an innocent person.

When they returned to the raid briefing they all settled in for a PowerPoint overview held in the training classroom. The narcs had taken a bunch of photos of the crooks, and the houses to be searched and wanted to make sure everybody was as familiar as possible with the place they'd been assigned to hit. Like all cops they knew that raids like this were dangerous enough when everybody knew their job and who the other cops involved were. Friendly fire incidents were rare in law enforcement but not unheard of, and with thirty officers involved it was important that everybody know what was happening. Lieutenant Jenkins, the commander over narcotics who technically supervised the gang unit, and Sergeant Glen gave everyone a handout with names and assignments.

Jenkins explained that their undercover officer had hooked up with a crook after being introduced several weeks ago by an informant. A couple of small buys of meth had been made and they followed the crook to another house where he got the dope. They believed based on utility usage (the electric bill was huge) and traffic coming and going from the second house, that it might be a lab operation. The guys assigned that place had a hazardous material trained narc team attached to them because of the dangerous chemicals and the threat of explosion or fire. Cam and Bobby had the other house along with a few more gang unit members and a couple of narcs because the crooks that lived there were ganged up.

As Cam was standing up from the briefing Todd Wilms leaned over toward him and said, "I think J-Tra's sister might be dating the mope that lives at the house we're hitting. His phone number was in her address book and cell phone. They've also been seen together a couple of times. I hope I get to stuff that bitch in a jail cell just to get big brother's attention."

Every time Cam talked with Todd he said to himself, "I'm glad that testosterone-fueled ape is on my side."

When Bobby and Cam were in the locker room getting their raid clothes and equipment on, Bobby looked at Cam and said, "You seem a little preoccupied there, big guy. Problem?"

Cam said, "No, I'm good. I'm just wondering how we can put all this separate stuff together to make some kind of big bust like a conspiracy to traffic dope and girls case against these schmucks." In reality, Cam wasn't that good, no matter how many excuses he made. This ax hanging over his head was hard to ignore and it tended to push all other thoughts aside. He needed a new mindset. You could do amazing things if you could get your head to cooperate. The problem was, Cam's mind had a mind of its own.

Everybody had their body armor on with the ballistic plates inserted. The point men even had Kevlar helmets. Radios were all set to a separate network and when units were in position they called in their ready status. They would go on the Lieutenant's command when the final drug deal went down with the undercover cop. He was wired and under visual surveillance. The plan was to serve the search warrants even if the buy fell apart, which is frequently the case. Often the seller wouldn't have the dope or stretched the deal out because he was trying for more money or he was just worried about it being a set up. The department narcs had too much time, money and manpower tied up on this case to continue it till later. The Lieutenant said they would take what they found and file the other buys with the D.A.s office.

Cam and Bobby were assigned to cover the rear of the house on Figaro Street. They would try to make entry but their first priority was to secure anybody who broke out the back.

Both of them had shotguns but decided against using them because their position often required grabbing suspects and cuffing them. The problem was what do you do with a shotgun when you're taking some suspect to the ground? You can't lay it down and you can't sling it on your back easily in an arrest take down.

They sat in their car with a line of sight on the driveway they had to run down to get to the back door and they waited. This was always the stressful moment of a search warrant raid. The initial rush to get in the house was the dangerous part. You were entering someone else's territory. They knew the lay out and if they saw you coming you were a sitting duck. Every house has a dozen ambush spots if you know where they are. Cam had often thought how easy it would be to shoot someone trying to get into his house, if he knew they were coming.

Cam was watching Bobby out of the corner of his eye and knew that he often said a little silent prayer before he did raids like this so as they waited for the signal from the Lieutenant he asked Bobby, "Did you include me when you asked the big cop in the sky for protection?"

Bobby said, "Always."

Cam said, "How bout I throw some chicken bones in the air and stick a pin in my doper doll before we jump?" Bobby just shook his head and Cam thought, I'm back.

The Lieutenant hit the radio and said, "All units, Now! Execute!" The raid was on.

Bobby and Cam jumped out of the car together and unholstered their Glocks as they ran across the street. They were a few houses down so they jumped a three-foot hedge and went as close to the neighbor's houses as possible before they hit the crook's driveway. The front door entry team was just knocking on the door as Cam and Bobby rounded the back of the house. They positioned themselves on either side of the back door attempting to get as much cover as possible from any gun fire. There were thick shrubs on either side of the door that made getting to the side difficult, but it wasn't wise to stand in front of doors so they pushed their bodies into the bushes.

As they waited they could hear the front door team announce, "Police Officer-Search Warrant." All hell broke loose in the house. People were running and screaming everywhere. There appeared to me more crooks present than originally thought. Bobby kicked the back door but it only budged a little so he stepped back and got a good plant with his other foot and nailed it harder this time right next to the lock. The door gave way and Cam went in first as Bobby was regaining his balance. Cam had a two-handed grip on his extended weapon as he looked over the gun barrel. Bobby was hot on Cam's heels and he paused with Cam at a side bedroom door because they'd heard something. Bobby put a hand on Cam's back so he could tell when they were moving forward without having to look. This was where partners that knew each other well really clicked. Cam knew why Bobby was resting his hand on his back and also knew that Bobby's gun wasn't pointed at him. Trust and confidence in your partner was critical at moments like this.

As they stepped in front of the door they both saw a gang punk all decked out in red clothes with a red bandana and an autoloader turned sideways in his hand. Bobby instinctively shoved Cam forward as he jumped past the door. The punk fired two rounds at Cam but only hit Bobby with one round right over the kidney. Both Cam and Bobby went down in the hallway past the shooter's door as Todd Wilms went by them coming from the other direction. Wilms stuck his shotgun around the corner of the shooter's bedroom door and without even looking to see what was there he extended both arms in front of the door as he pumped four rounds of .00 buck into the room. Each round had nine .32 caliber pellets which laid down a deadly spray of lead. Only a muscled-up animal like Todd could fire a bucking shotgun accurately held out at full arm extension. He dropped his empty shotgun and had his Glock out before the shotgun hit the ground. As he did a quick flash look, putting his head in and out of the doorway quickly, he saw the shooter down in the room. He then stuck his head back around the corner and assessed that the crook was no longer holding the gun and looked dead. He looked down at Cam and Bobby and found that they both were getting up seemingly uninjured. Todd went into the crook's bedroom to see if the shooter was alive. He kicked away the crook's gun, which was lying on the floor, flipped him over on his back and took his carotid pulse. Cam went immediately to Bobby's side where he saw the torn vest and pulled up the side of the vest to see how bad Bobby was hurt. There was some busted skin and a little blood from the blunt trauma impact but the slug was still in the body armor.

Cam looked at Bobby and said, "That's going to hurt like a bitch tomorrow."

Bobby said through clenched teeth, "It hurts like a bitch right now."

Cam thought, so that's what it takes for Bobby to swear: getting shot. Damn, I really owe him one now.

Officer Randolph Keen was in the living room pointing a 12-gauge shotgun at a gang member who had been sleeping on a couch. A cheap revolver was lying on the floor next to the couch and the crook was looking at it and then back at Keen.

As Keen pointed his shotgun at the crook he said in his best Dirty Harry voice, "You've got to ask yourself one question. Do I feel lucky? Well, do ya, punk?"

Apparently, the punk didn't feel lucky because he just put his hands, on top of his head and waited. He also didn't recognize the movie quote because he wasn't born yet when that movie was released.

All the gang members were secured in cuffs and relocated to the living room. They were all told to sit on the floor while the officers determined who the owner of the house was so he could be read the warrant. J-Tra's sister wasn't there but three members of his gang were. This appeared to be their main connection for dope.

As Bobby was looking at the dead gang member who Wilms shot, he called Cam over.

Bobby said, "Recognize him?" Cam shrugged. "This is Jose', the punk you pantsed in front of the junior high."

Cam took a long look at the corpse with a direct shotgun blast to the chest, and said, "Well, I guess I don't have to worry about him trying to shoot me anymore. Although he probably has three brothers, two uncles and twelve cousins who'll want to fill in for him."

Bobby said, "Ya, with any luck they'll try to shoot Wilms, which would be the mistake that gets their whole family wiped out."

The narcotics Lieutenant told Sergeant Glen to have all his boys do reports on the shooting and forward a copy to him. He was happy with the raid because now, under California case law, he could charge the gang members and people who controlled the house with homicide because someone (their buddy) died as a result of their criminal act.

He might not get all the way through the courts but it was a good starting place.

Wilms got a few days off till the shooting investigation was over and the Sergeant told Cam to take Bobby by the hospital for a checkup even though he looked fine. The ID guys met him there to photograph the injury for court evidence. They tagged and logged his vest with the slug in it.

As Cam and Bobby waited for the X-rays to come back Cam told Bobby, "I think your prayer was defective because you got shot."

Bobby said, "On the contrary, I think it worked because you were saved and I'm not really hurt."

Cam told him, "You true believers would call the sinking of the Titanic a prayer answered because they did save a couple of people."

Bobby just smiled at Cam and said, "Well, partner, at least I was able to save your life."

As Cam's jaws locked up Bobby, who was fighting a big smile, turned his head away because he knew he was driving Cam crazy.

You'll Know Someday

Lieutenant Raymond Jenkins was not always as polished a gentleman as he currently appeared. While he and Sergeant Glen were coming up through the ranks, police work was done a little differently. In those good old days, when a prisoner took a swing at a cop he went to jail via the hospital. Law Enforcement thought it necessary to discourage such conduct. You wanted to make it known that assaulting a cop had unpleasant consequences. Booze you confiscated was not destroyed, but donated to the departmental Christmas party and everything was discounted by merchants for a cop. Meals were half price in restaurants and motorcycle officers even took a patrol car out just before Christmas so they could carry away all the gratuities. A few cops would come to work to sleep on the night watch, if they could get a buddy to cover for them or at least wake them up for calls. Professionalism wasn't as demanding as it is today.

Jenkins had to remember that whenever he talked with Glen, because Glen was one of the few old timers that knew all of the Lieutenant's secrets.

He needed to talk with Sergeant Glen regarding rumors he'd heard about a few gang squad members' activities. He had a big promotion coming up that could be squashed by any indication that he was lax in controlling his special units. Career success in Law Enforcement meant not making waves for the Chief. It wasn't a system that rewarded innovation and success as much as it was an animal that didn't like surprises. By the time cops got to the higher levels of their department, their overwhelming job attribute was that they caused zero problems for the Chief.

∞

While Cam was busy cranking out the inevitable piles of paperwork a raid and fatal shooting required of an officer, there was another totally different investigation just getting started.

Mountain View detective Alex Martinez was what other cops called a dogged investigator. Where other detectives would move on, Alex dug in. He didn't let boredom or case load or any outside pressures detour him from his objective. He was a skinny, small framed, 35-year-old with a wife and five kids. As a result, he had little money, a full house, a ratted-out car and a tendency to put in a lot of overtime in the detective assignment he now had for the last three years. His buddies kidded him about working so much because he had so many kids to feed and because he couldn't get into the bathroom at his house. They were about 90% right. At least he had some control over something when he went to work. He could not say the same about life on the home front. He had four girls starting at fifteen years old going down to four and one boy eighteen months old. His wife told him that she was done. He had his boy and she had her tubes tied. Some of his fellow officers described Alex as whipped at home which was why he was such a hard-ass at work.

Alex loved his detective assignment but he had come by it the hard way. He was transferred from patrol after an unfortunate shooting incident. His supervisors had advised the Chief that Alex was close to having a PTSD event and needed a break from the streets.

It all started while on patrol one cool summer evening a few years back. Alex had been assigned to handle a call involving a mother who ran out of medication for her schizophrenic son. She was told by the county health clinic that they couldn't help her after hours on a weekend so she should contact the police department. When Alex arrived at the house he found the twenty-three-year-old son had grabbed a butcher knife and crawled up on top of a sheet metal tool shed located in his back yard. A back up officer and his sergeant were with him as he tried to talk with the hallucinating kid. It became apparent that the communication was only one way with this very sick young man. The call had dragged on for an hour and they were getting some heat from the watch commander via dispatch to wrap it up and get back in service. The Sergeant instructed Alex to take the left flank with his Glock at a low ready which means out of its holster but aimed at the ground below the young man. He ordered the other officer to use his Taser and shoot the kid. It would hit him with 50,000 volts but not do any permanent damage, just knock him out long enough to disarm him and get him cuffed so he could be transported to the mental ward.

As Alex waited in his low ready position, he prepared himself to holster and catch this guy when he was Tasered so he didn't break his neck falling off the shed roof. He had a flash vision of seeing park rangers tranquilize bears out of a tree.

When the Taser was fired it didn't work correctly. The batteries were low so it stuck into the kid and administered a low-voltage shock. It wasn't enough to knock him out but it was plenty strong enough to hurt him. He pulled out the darts and attacked the officers in a full paranoid assault. Alex's role in this tactical situation was cover for the Taser officer. He was supposed to protect the officer, because he had a one-shot Taser in his hand and didn't have a way of protecting himself.

Alex aimed at the young man and screamed for him to stop several times but it was doubtful the extremely mentally ill kid understood. What was clear was that someone would get stabbed by a big knife if Alex didn't fire. He considered for a split second, firing a wounding shot because he was that confident in his firearm skills but remembered all the law and procedures taught at the police academy. Shooting to wound is not allowed. The U.S. Supreme court has made it clear that if you didn't need to shoot for center body mass to stop a suspect than you didn't need to shoot at all. The department always instructed that if you shoot someone you aim for the center of the chest or head. Nothing else. If you violate policy you stand alone in lawsuits and possibly on criminal charges.

Alex hesitated long enough as he mulled over his options that the Sergeant yelled at him, "Fire!"

Alex did. He did a double tap and placed two rounds an inch apart in the young man's heart. As he fell to the ground with a hysterical mother running to hold him Alex knew there wasn't a need to even call an ambulance or administer first aid. He saw where the rounds hit and knew it was over.

The patrol Sergeant, a Viet Nam veteran who was a famous cynic on the department and who'd seen his share of these types of incidents, shrugged and said, "Another Village Pacified" as he radioed for the coroner and shooting review team. The comment hit Alex like a punch to the gut. His old man would only talk about his stint in Viet Nam with the Marine Corps when he was drunk. When he was good and loaded he'd talk about how they cleaned out entire villages including women, children and the elderly because they were designated free fire zones and enemy occupied on some map. He'd always finish the stories with a crying jag and the quote, "Another Village Pacified." Alex always wondered why his dad didn't just do the right thing instead of following orders. While he loved his dad, he couldn't completely respect him because he'd always been taught to do the right thing even if it cost you personally. His shooting of the mentally ill kid taught him the right thing is not always so easy to define.

After a couple of rocky months on patrol Alex was assigned to Detectives. His Sergeant told administration, "The kid has earned it and we owe it to him."

The Lieutenant handed Alex the investigation file that had been started on the two drugged girls that had been dropped off at the Mountain View hospital last week. He told him, "I've had informant rumors coming out of the narc squad that some cowboy cop did an off the record rescue in our city and I don't like that one bit. It looks like kidnapping, breaking and entering and maybe excessive force under the color of law. I want someone's ass in a cell over this. This vigilante conduct is not going to go on in my city."

There was very little to work with on this investigation as there were no decent witnesses and the victim/suspect girls had lawyered up and weren't cooperating. This just made Alex all the more determined to find out what the hell went on. At least he had one Ace up his sleeve. The Chief of security at the hospital was an ex-cop that he had worked with and maybe he could help break a few investigative leads free.

"Tom, Alex Martinez."

"Hi Alex, I thought you guys would be ringing my machine. How's it going at MVPD?"

Alex said, "Good as can be expected in the politically correct world of Yuppiesville."

Thomas Grant laughed and said, "So what's up?" Alex explained that he was assigned the two drugged girls case and was looking for some leads. "Ya, I thought you guys would be calling so I ran up the security tape on that night."

"Well, what's it show?"

"Not much. The guys covered up pretty well but he's not your common junkie dropping off an overdosed buddy. Come on over and I'll show it to you."

Alex said, "Tom, is there anything in the medical report that would help me?"

Tom paused for a moment and carefully selected his next few words. "As you know I'm not allowed to release confidential medical records without a subpoena or warrant. Why don't you come over and we'll talk." Alex knew that Tom would be reviewing the reports for helpful information but that he wouldn't be getting a copy without the legal paperwork. That was good enough. At least he'd know whether it was worth pursuing.

As Tom and Alex sat in the security office and watched the drop off of the two girls, Alex saw what Tom meant when he said this wasn't a junkie dropping off the girls. The guy moved quickly in an athletic style that didn't waste a step. He was obviously strong as he placed the girl in the chair with one hand and was giving instructions to the other girl. He drove a pickup truck away in a calm but quick manor that showed a cool demeanor. The truck looked like an older model F150 but he couldn't be sure what color because the video was in black and white and you couldn't see the plates because of the tail gate.

Tom said, "I think he's some kind of law enforcement?"

"Why do you think that, Tom?"

"Because, look at his right hip when I replay the part where he's bending over the chair."

There it was as plain as the nose on your face, a bulge on the right hip right above the belt. Every cop recognizes the distinctive bulge of an autoloader's gun butt. Not a gun shoved into a waist band like a gangster but a high-rise holster like a pro would wear.

Alex and Tom ran through the tape several times trying to see if they missed anything but after analyzing it to death couldn't come up with anything more. They weren't even sure what race or age the guy was. They estimated the size and weight based on the comparison with the wheel chair. Tom had even run up a reenactment of him getting the chair in front of the same camera and since he was six foot one and 220 lbs. they guessed their suspect to be at least six feet tall and 180 lbs.

Tom said, "Not much to go on."

Alex wasn't surprised and asked, "True, but what else you got on the girls?"

Tom motioned for them to go into his office away from the other security employees.

"The girls both had been sexually abused over a long period of time because there were new and old bruises and scabs. They had been slapped and hit repeatedly and one of them had two teeth knocked out. They both had a smorgasbord of STD's. They both had just been introduced to the needle. They had about four or five needle marks that looked to be less than a week old but none into the veins yet. So, whoever did it was still muscling the injections for fear of ODing them. They could have picked up the STDs from the needle or the rapes. It's a fucking miracle they didn't get AIDS. The doctors thought their prognosis for recovery was good if they got effective care and treatment. And it looks like they will because they're scheduled to go to a high-end rehab hospital next week."

Alex was quiet for a minute trying to figure out all that Tom had told him.

"Where are they going for rehab Tom?"

Tom smiled and said, "Colorado, for a taste of the Rocky Mountain High."

Alex just shook his head. This thing just kept getting better. He'd never get anything out of them. Nothing pissed him of more than being stonewalled by some slick attorney.

∞

Kat was coming out of the fog. Her memory was a little sketchy about a few things but she did remember most of what had happened to her. She was a little sick but guessed that was the drug withdrawal. Strangely enough she didn't want dope. Sick or not, it felt good to not be in that drug induced fog. She thought her parents' plan to send them to rehab was largely unnecessary but then figured it couldn't hurt since she needed to get her shit together mentally. She also knew it would make life easier on Cam if she was gone for a while. Her Uncle Jimmy explained the tactic to her and asked for her help. She felt like she owed Cam her life and understood the tremendous risk he took getting her out of the gang house. She always liked Cam and had a crush on him when she was younger. When she saw his face the night he rescued her from the drug house it was like a fantasy where the knight saves the princess and she remembered being swept away by the feeling of complete relief when she saw him. She instantly knew she would be saved because Cam was, in her eyes, invincible. She would do anything for him she could and hoped she'd be able to thank him someday for saving her life.

Why had she gotten herself into this mess? How stupid was she, to think she was going to be more independent on her own by rejecting all her parents' rules? All she did was make herself more dependent and put her life in the hands of some truly evil people who were using her like an animal. The only way she could deal with the sexual assault and being handed around like a party bong was to not think about it. She was a little fearful that the psychologist at the rehab center wouldn't let her ignore that part of the last several weeks

Her current doctor, Sue Cline, was a particularly blunt and aggressive Jewish woman who explained all her medical issues without mincing words. She came to their shared room one morning where the two girls were lying in bed and explained that they had been lucky because all of their diseases were treatable and their injuries would heal. She also said that their addiction was no deeper than a prescription usage and should be easily put behind them if they were smart enough and mature enough to take advantage of the rehab opportunities given them. She said if they did not, she would see them in the autopsy room in a couple of years because that's where all drug users eventually end up. All of a sudden, all the dope lectures and warnings from adults hit home. This wasn't abstract somebody else stuff anymore. This was real. It was her life and it was her responsibility.

∞

Alex's first thought was which one of our officers fits the description of the mystery hero. He figured he'd start the elimination process with narcs and gang squad members because they were operating in that area of crime, then move to general detectives and then patrol. As he started to work his way through the number of guys who fit the physical description he found it easier than he thought. Twenty years ago, all the cops on the force would have been a close physical match, but legal changes allowed minorities and female cops into the department as well as smaller officers. He only had to eliminate seven cops from the first batch. Upon checking they all had court or were on duty handling investigation when this thing went down, so he moved to cops on detective assignments and patrol. After a week's work, none of them looked good for the rescue either. This damn case was hitting a stone wall. He guessed he'd start looking at retired cops who worked as Private Investigators in the area. Maybe one of them was his hero. He didn't even want to think about neighboring jurisdictions because there were literally thousands of officers in the San Francisco Bay area.

All PIs had to be licensed by the city, so Alex started down the list. For once the City of Mountain View made it easy for him. There was an actual photo with a physical description of every PI applicant. He had five agencies to talk with after the elimination process. He was coming up dry on every visit until he contacted "Davis Investigations." The owner was a retired cop who had left the San Jose Police Department ten years prior on a medical injury. Officer Charles Davis was responding to a window smash burglary at a clothing store one night ten years ago when a low IQ parolee stepped out of the window display carrying a 12-gauge shotgun. Charles and the burglar exchanged fire at a distance of fifteen feet. The crook died from a 9mm head wound from Charles's handgun and Charles lost three fingers on his left hand from a shotgun blast. Fortunately, his trigger finger got some protection from the trigger guard. If a ticket book in a leather holder hadn't been in his left inside jacket pocket against departmental policy (they thought it looked too officious) he'd have been dead. He was medically retired with a fat pension and given some Worker's Comp money to retrain for a new career. He took PI classes and started his own business.

Alex didn't know him, but he hoped the fraternity of Law Enforcement would buy him some cooperation. When Alex asked Charles about his whereabouts the night of the rescue Charles had a solid alibi because he was attending a court trial as a witness in Los Angeles that week.

Charles casually asked Alex what this was all about and Alex said, "I'm looking into the two girls that were rescued from a Nortenos gang last week."

Charles quietly said, "I can't talk about that case. Client confidentiality, you know?"

Alex tried not to show his surprise. If this guy was hired to investigate something to do with these two girls then he may have a starting point. He knew Charles wouldn't share any information with him because if a client ever found out that a PI betrayed a confidential trust, his business was dead. But maybe he could get some information by looking at some other sources. All PI's needed a law enforcement contact. So much of what they did came from sources that had record access to police department files. It was usually a good buddy from when they worked at the PD but it was a touchy proposition because a cop could get fired for accessing data for someone not authorized to have it. That's why it had to be a real good buddy.

Alex thanked Charles and went back to the PD to start making calls. If this PI was investigating the missing girls then it would be likely that whoever rescued them was in contact with the PI or his client at some point. Alex tried to think of any officer he knew that would have been around 10 years ago when Charles was on the SJPD, but he came up dry because a lot of the department members were hired only a few years ago. He told his Sergeant what he was up to and the Sergeant told him to talk with a detective by the name of Don Harper. Harper transferred laterally to Mountain View a couple of years ago for a promotion.

Harper nodded his head as he listened to Alex's story and said, "Joseph Silva is your boy. He and Charlie were partners for years and I know Joe used to moonlight for Charlie off the books when he first started his PI business. That's his source." Alex thanked him profusely and phoned the SJPD to see what shift Joe Silva was working. He was going to have a nice long talk with Joe.

CONVERGING AT HIGH SPEED

Cam decided that there were two important things he needed to do instead of worrying about things he couldn't control.

Get on J-Tra's case big time and see how things were with Jane.

He wasn't sure how he was going to do either but he'd be damned if he was going to let things unfold at a snail's pace. He needed to make shit happen on both fronts.

Cam and Bobby went to their old thinking spot at the park where they would eat their lunch when they were on patrol. As they were snacking out of a small ice chest, Cam told Bobby about his two immediate goals. He wasn't sure why he told Bobby about Jane but figured it couldn't hurt because Bobby generally had a way of giving good advice when it came to people.

Bobby just nodded his head and said, "Well I thought you were out of your mind when you let her get away but I've only got one thing to say about you restarting that relationship." Cam waited and after a moment Bobby said, "You might have one more shot at her but she's not the kind of person who will accept half steps or you thinking it over."

Cam just nodded and said, "Ya, I know."

They sat there sipping on their Gatorade for a few minutes then Bobby said, "Now, about our gang buddies and Mr. Travaldos. What exactly did you have in mind?

Cam said, "I'm not completely sure but I think the best way to hurt that asshole is to hit him with a search warrant where he least expects it. I think we need to rattle a few informant cages and see if any of the other squad members can help. Maybe with some other guys helping we'll have enough to get a warrant signed. Everybody's been chipping away at J-Tra, we just have to become the clearing station for all this loose data and put it all together. And not worry about it being a squeaky clean legal document.

Bobby said, "It's a plan. It sounds like a high-flying Cam plan, but it is a plan. Let's go see how Lupe is doing."

Lupe was difficult to locate because her pimp was working her for the gang and had her doing tricks all day and all night. When Bobby finally got her to call him back he told her it was an emergency and he needed to see her now. She relented and gave him a meeting time in a couple of hours at a city park on the good side of town where her class of people didn't go.

Bobby played it low key and talked about other stuff to try and get her to relax. He asked her how she knew about this park and she said she came here with her sister and her kids, so Bobby asked about the nieces and nephews. She melted when she talked about them and it was apparent that she wanted kids of her own even though it seemed like a wish for something impossible in her current life. There was something incongruent with her wish for a family and the way Lupe looked with her too short shorts, tube top, poorly done ink on her shoulder and at least six ear studs.

Cam watched in mild admiration as Bobby did what he could not. Bobby had the patience and genuine concern to establish a relationship with this lost soul. Bobby told her he had a couple of opportunities for her to think about and he needed her help. He started by telling her the opportunities were there for her no matter if she helped him or not, but that he really needed her.

She leaned back against the edge of the picnic table and put her elbows on the top. Her face showed a skeptic's guarded patience.

"First," he said, "I know you wanted to become a hair stylist and work in that business and maybe someday have your own place. I remembered you mentioning that to me when we talked before. But then all this crazy gang and dope stuff got you off track. You said, maybe you could find a nice guy and have some kids of your own. Well, I talked with a lady who in my ward, church, and she'd be willing to hire you and help you get the license training if you're interested. That's going to mean you getting into rehab and staying clean but I think this might be the out you're looking for."

Lupe just stared at Bobby for a few seconds and was trying to size him up. "Why would she do that for me when she don't even know me?"

Bobby was stumbling over his words to try to explain how his church worked and Cam interrupted. "Lupe, Bobby's people are a bunch of Jesus freaks. They help people because God told them too."

Lupe looked back from Cam toward Bobby then slowly nodded her head realizing that Bobby was telling her the truth.

What Cam and Bobby didn't know was that their timing couldn't have been better. Lupe's pimp had just set up a trick for her a couple of hours ago with fat, smelly, brutal man at least thirty years older than her. The trick had slapped her around, then bit her breast and back while he was holding a fist full of her hair. When he was finished she turned around to find him removing a ripped condom that she was sure he'd ripped open when he rolled her over. When a John doesn't care about a condom it's usually because he's already got something and not worried about getting something else. She was so humiliated, hurt, and angry that fear of the gang was not the deterrent it once was.

She looked at Bobby and Cam for a minute and said, "If I give you guys something can you keep me out of it and make sure nobody knows?

Bobby said, "Yes, I swear it."

She added, "No court, nothing written down?

Cam said, "You have our word," as he raised his right hand.

She stared at both of them for about 10 seconds with the only sound being chirping birds and distant traffic and said, "Okay, J-Tra is getting pressed hard by the Nuestra Familia big boys for back money he owes them. They treat this bunch of Nortenos like a Burger King that ain't been selling enough burgers. He ain't doing shit compared to other gangs in the bay area. When you guys fuck with him it's causing him grief. He can't work new girls he'd been getting ready because someone popped them free. You hit his dope connection house and even though you didn't get much, you made his connection stay away for a while to see how hot J-Tra really is. And now he's afraid to use a cell phone because you copped all those numbers when you raided his momma's house. He even thinks there may be a rat on the inside because those two girls that got away were hid real good. Shit, they weren't even in the city. He's got to make a big score on dope to cover the losses, so he's setting up a big-ass sale of crank to some bikers out of Portland. There's gunna be a bunch of dope and a bunch of money and a bunch of guns."

Realizing that this was the break they'd been waiting for, Cam asked, "When is this thing going to happen, Lupe?"

"I think late next week because the connection don't trust J-Tra and wants to be close by when the deal's done to get his cut. And the Portland bikers got to get down here and set the buy up so they don't get ripped off. Everybody's paranoid because they all know everyone's a thief."

Bobby said, "Lupe, how do you know all this stuff?"

She smiled and said, "Because this pack of shit-heads like to brag when they fuck and they drink too much. They're all trying to act like they're big shots and know everything and they think I'm just some simple whore who can't hurt anybody. When they pass me around at their parties I listen and put it all together."

Bobby and Cam got a few more details to try to tighten up the information, then they cut Lupe loose with two phone numbers written on a scrap of paper she could stuff in the bottom of her purse. This time they were worried about J-Tra being paranoid enough to search her for phone numbers and they didn't want a repeat of the "Dawn" incident so they altered the numbers a little. Neither number would get her anybody anyone knew they explained, but if you took the first three numbers from one and the last four from the other you'd get Cam's or Bobby's cell. They thanked her for the information and admonished her to be cool and not act any different than before.

When Bobby and Cam left Lupe, they contacted a few other informants to see if they could come up with any helpful information. They were careful to not let on they knew about the big score pending because they didn't want J-Tra to know there was a leak. The only help they got verifying Lupe's story was from Ray. He told them something big was coming up but he didn't know what because J-Tra and the other guys weren't talking a bunch. He thought it involved some of the older Nuestra Familia members because he's heard a few guys worrying about how violent they were and how they treated the gang members like hired help. Cam left Ray with the suggestion to keep his ears open but not ask any questions for fear of getting burnt. All this information was no good unless they could nail down the location of this deal. It's a big city, and as of now it could happen anywhere.

Bobby and Cam decided they'd split up some duties. Cam was going to try to find all the homes and property that the gang had connections to while Bobby was going to talk with other investigators working gangs and drugs to see if they could help add any details to this sketchy story. The problem the two partners had was that the 4th amendment required specific knowledge of the persons and places to be searched. It required first-hand information before a warrant could be issued and Lupe's story didn't have many names or places. Not enough for a search warrant.

Cam knew where he was going to start hunting for more information: the house he'd sprung the two girls from. There had to be an agent involved and if the gang used the same agent for other purchases he might find the place where the deal was going to go down. That address was known to other cops but they didn't know what he knew, that it was a safe house for training whores.

Bobby knew where he wanted to start also. The gang investigator's meeting might break something loose. He had to be careful how much he shared because he didn't want to blow this case by letting too much information out. Another narc or gang squad member might say the wrong thing when questioning an informant and scare the crooks away. But he was curious about these two girls that Lupe said got rescued and he suspected that Cam had something to do with it because Cam didn't want her to elaborate and looked nervous as hell when the subject came up.

∞

Alex was in luck because Joe Silva was working a swing shift on patrol so he could crawl into his patrol car and gently put the screws to him. He was also in luck because his mother-in-law had planned a birthday party with the whole family, all fifty-five of them, to celebrate her other daughter's 30th birthday. This way he could whip in, have a slice of cake and get the hell out of there with the excuse of "duty calls."

When he got into the car with Silva they chatted about the department and what a crazy political organization it was. Joe was slightly famous in Law Enforcement circles because he was number one on the sergeant's list when he had the misfortune of shooting a Mexican male who had beat the crap out of his wife. This violated the first natural law of police shootings, "If you're going to kill someone with your duty weapon make sure he's a white male." The suspect was drunk and charged Joe and his partner with a knife so the legality of the shooting wasn't an issue. The problem was that this was the third departmental killing of a Hispanic in a month and the ethnic community demanded someone's head. Joe got passed over for promotion and assigned to patrol the outskirts of town on the night shift for the next six months.

When he protested the assignment and not getting his stripes, the Lieutenant told him that "in this political environment with a Mexican councilman up for reelection you best shut up and wait for all this to blow over."

When Joe contacted his union representative about being passed over and reassigned the union rep said, "Joe, this one of those situations where you might win the battle but lose the war."

He could fight for his rights but it would be front page news and cause the city manager major headaches. He'd be sure to pay for it one way or the other. So, he choked it down and took the punishment.

This was the real truth about police work today. You were judged by someone's cell phone video or the media's interview with a suspect's mother. Nobody waited for a real investigation because that took time and network media had to compete with the on-line news. When cops didn't talk, under advice of counsel, the media filled in their version of truth. The police department always ordered officers not to talk with the press because of their civil liability, but the 5th estate didn't care. The public hates a vacuum so the media is always glad to fill it with something that would ratchet up emotion because emotion was better for ratings than logic. There was a reason PBS had lower viewer ratings then the networks. In the earlier days of law enforcement, it was understood that cops weren't perfect, but in today's world there was no room for mistakes. If administrators could cover for a good cop and correct any training errors they would, but if the public demanded a head they swallowed their ethics and served Head Ala Platter.

In Joe's case his Lieutenant told him, "We'll make it right as soon as we can." Joe was still bitter about the fucking he'd received but after venting a bit to Alex, Joe's curiosity got the best of him.

He told Alex, "You didn't come out here this evening to talk departmental gossip. So, what's on your mind?"

Alex responded by saying, "Okay, here's my problem. I'm investigating two girls being dumped at our hospital by a guy who looks like a cop. They were kidnapped and drugged and as far as I can tell getting prepped to be gang prostitutes. And nobody knows shit. Your buddy at Davis investigation has some info but can't share it so I'm here asking you for help since you helped him out on some records research. This part of Alex's little speech was a bluff but he was almost positive Joe had helped Charlie get some background information because if he were in Charlie's position he would have put the touch on Joe.

Joe thought for a moment and being a veteran IA (Internal Affairs) survivor said, "What makes you think I helped Charlie with this investigation?"

Alex responded, "Joe, we both know that if I file this thing as an open I.A. the department will do a computer sweep to see who accessed the information and some people could get in trouble for sharing confidential records with an unauthorized person. Now I don't want to bring that kind of grief down on any fellow cop over bullshit like this but I need some answers and if I don't get some help here I'm left with little choice."

Joe sized up Alex and decided to trust him because he knew how pissed off cops got when they thought someone was stonewalling them.

"I looked at some records on gang members and specifically an asshole called J-Tra. His last name is Travaldos. He runs the local Nortenos crew. Charlie was trying to locate a girl for the family and see what her activities were with the gang. I guess she was some little spoiled rich bitch who'd run off with a gang boyfriend. I didn't copy anything for him. All I did was tell him who the players were on the gang and what we knew about their activities."

Alex nodded and asked, "Did he say who hired him?"

Joe smiled and said, "The infamous Jimmy Scanlon."

Alex thanked Joe for his help and reassured him that he didn't see any fallout from this conversation. The one thing he didn't need is some other cop hot mouthing him around the PD. If you're going to pick a fight with another cop you better make sure it's worth it because the blowback could get ugly.

If this thing was all about San Jose gangs the best place to get information was a quiet visit to the next regional Gang Investigator's meeting. His mind was working on several possibilities. Did Jimmy Scanlon hire someone to rescue the girls? And why didn't he just use Law Enforcement?

∞

Information flows both ways in the relationship between government and private business. The public was always getting worked up about government intruding into personal privacy, but people turn around and give huge volumes of intimate information to private companies. Then, all law enforcement had to do was to go get it from them. Cam knew that the really efficient way to find who bought and sold real estate was to access an agent who could get the records for him. A bunch of guys he knew on the force used an officer's sister. She was an agent with a local company and was a major badge bunny to boot. Cam had talked with her a couple of times about property he was interested in and she'd helped him on a previous investigation so he knew this wouldn't be a tough sell. Cam caught her at her office and she told him to drop by and they'd talk. He explained what he was looking for which essentially was any property owned by the Nortenos or Nuestra Familia. He gave her a list of the players' names and their parents and other family members' names. He also gave her addresses he knew that were used by the gang in case there was a different name they were using. He particularly pointed out the Mountain View house where he rescued the girls.

She told him that this might take a while but that she'd call him soon with whatever she found. She also asked him for a date, which put him in the position of rejecting the woman he'd just asked for help or saying yes, so he told her it sounded great but that it would have to be in a couple of weeks because of this gang case. As he walked away he knew it was a lie because he was thinking about Jane but then thought, you never know, Jane could tell him to take a flying leap.

∞

As Bobby sat in his chair around a long conference table with two dozen other gang investigators, he thought he recognized most of the cops except a couple. As Alex Martinez from Mountain View introduced himself he noticed an odd look from the other Mountain View gang investigator, which told Bobby that maybe Alex wasn't really supposed to attend this get together. Bobby presented a few facts and investigation leads but didn't mention the new information from Lupe because he didn't want any leaks and really didn't have enough to be creditable. When everyone was taking a coffee break he overheard Todd Wilms talking with Alex Martinez. Alex was asking him if he knew the cop that was a good buddy of Jimmy Scanlon's.

Todd answered, "Oh, you mean Cam, Cam Michaelson. He and Jimmy were buddies in high school. Bobby could see the name register on Alex's face. It was like he just got box seats to the World Series.

Alex asked, "Is he a big guy, like 6'2" and 180 lbs.?"

Todd answered, "Ya, about that, and a bad motherfucking karate dude too." Alex and Todd talked about some other unrelated stuff for a minute and then Alex walked away.

Bobby located the other Mountain View investigator who was surprised at Alex being there and said, "I didn't recognize the other guy from your shop. Is he working gangs now?"

The investigator said, "No, I don't know why he came. He mostly works sensitive stuff out of the chief's office like IA's on other officers or sometimes cases that nobody else has time for. He's a bull dog. Not sure why he's hanging around here. I thought he was assigned to the case of those two girls that got rescued from a drug house. He's got more kids than a horny Mormon and a couple of them are teenage daughters, so maybe he just wanted to get away from the house. He's not a particularly nice guy."

Bobby let the Mormon crack go because he had a couple of things on his mind: one regarding a house where a deal was going down and the other a partner who looked to be in deep trouble.

∞

Cam got the call from the real estate agent two days later. "Hi Cam, this is Lisa. Can you come by and we'll talk about this stuff I ran up for you?"

Cam said, "Sure, 1:00 work for you?"

"Fine, handsome, see you then."

Lisa was dressed in a light see through blouse and a short, tight skirt and wearing way too much perfume when they met. She pulled an office chair over to her desk so Cam could see her computer screen as she scrolled through the data. In spite of her touching Cam far too much she researched this project like a true pro.

As they went over the ownership of several homes and rental agreements on some houses it became apparent that the gang and their family mostly rented houses but the older members owned a couple. Lisa found the best lead when she checked on the recent sale of the house on South El Monte.

She told Cam, "The sales proceeds went to a guy who's married to one of J-Tra's cousins. His name doesn't appear after that but a house was purchased on

Meadow View Drive in San Jose a few days later by a name you gave me and the deposit/down payment was for exactly the same amount as the sales check on the El Monte house."

Cam said, "Looks like the first place wasn't secret anymore so they thought they'd come back to San Jose under another name. Too bad J-Tra's sister wrote this guy's name in her address book. I might not have ever found it. Thanks, Lisa, you've been a big help. Now don't say a word about this because it wouldn't do to have these boys know anything about you, okay?"

She said, "No shit."

He promised, "I'll call you," as he gathered the paperwork and headed for the door.

THE ELUSIVE MR. X

As Cam started to get his thoughts together in preparation for a search warrant, he thought about his advanced officer narcotics training. He'd had an instructor who worked with the famous L.A.P.D. narc, Commander Joe Gunn. This instructor started his search warrant lectures by handing out a transcript of a Joe Gunn lecture.

"The thing cops love about search warrants is that they usually don't require an informant to appear in court. If you arrest someone for a dope sales or sex trafficking you have to produce a victim or witness, but with a search warrant you're only charging the crook with what you find in his house or car. No witness is necessary because you're only charging someone with what they have in their possession. The crime is possession. One other nice feature of a search warrant is cops have the legal privilege to **not** reveal the identity of their informant. This drives defense attorneys nuts. California Evidence Code section 1040 (all states have a similar section) says that a peace officer in performance of his duties can refuse to identify his informant in court."

The instructor continued reading from Commander Gunn's lecture. "Attorneys will attempt to get the informant's name by asking a witness officer if Joe Blow is the informant, at which time the cop, from the witness stand, will turn to the judge and say, Your Honor I claim my privilege under 1040 of the Evidence Code. The judge will stop the court proceeding and ask the officer to come into chambers. Judges can ask for the informant's name or not. They can ask for the informant in a private meeting, but in most cases, they will simply ask what role your informant played and whether they were a material witness to the innocence of the defendant. Usually, judges return to the bench not knowing who the informant is and tell defense council that the informant can't shed any light on the defense's case, so move on and don't ask about the informant's identity. If a judge does think the informant could offer evidence that would help the defense he can order the officer to reveal the informant. If the officer still refuses to do so, the case will be dismissed but the informant remains secret."

This bit of legal obstruction was not lost on Cam. Cops can be devious at times. Attorneys use every trick in the book and occasionally invent some new ones, so why shouldn't cops? One example of that deviousness Cam remembered was the old timer's stories about how a batch of search warrants got served right after a major crook ODed and every cop who was forced to reveal their informant's identity said, "It was poor old dead Willy. Ain't it a shame he can't testify." The fact that you're not required to reveal your informants is often too tempting to resist. Every cop in this country can tell you the names of several crooks that are walking free in their jurisdiction because there's not enough evidence to get into their house or business. An imaginary Mr. X can solve that problem for you.

Cam knew that the downside of using an imaginary Mr. X is that if a cop or innocent baby gets killed on the raid or you discover Jimmy Hoffa, your department is REALLY going to want you to ID your informant so the case doesn't get dismissed.

But he tried not to sweat the unlikely and it was getting close to crunch time.

Somehow, he felt that if he could get J-Tra busted, and his operation shut down, it would solve most of his current problems. He wasn't sure how he arrived at that conclusion, but throughout his whole life taking decisive action seemed a better course than waiting for things to unfold naturally.

The location of the buy seemed fairly certain and could be verified by surveillance as the case moved along. J-Tra couldn't use any of the other houses because they were all too hot, so the new home had to be the place where the buy was going down. Cam knew who the players were, at least locally, but he didn't have enough legal probable cause to get a warrant, so he was going to need a little help from his imaginary friend. He would have to do the warrant himself because Bobby was such a boy scout he wouldn't go along with stretching the truth and he needed to start writing it soon because the drug deal was likely to go down in the next few days. When you were putting together a big warrant like this it required a bit of lead time to get all your people and logistics in place. When the out of town people got here, the deal would be done fast because all the crooks knew the danger in hanging around a town you don't know with incriminating evidence like dope, guns, or huge amounts of cash in your trunk.

Cam knew the key to any lie was to tell it around a partial truth so it seemed feasible.

Lupe could be the information source to sketch a warrant framework around and Mrs. X, soon to be Mr. X, would fill in the rest. Her statement about the dope deal would have to be stretched beyond her personal knowledge to include hearing the principles talk about the deal and witnessing other deals go down and of course she would have to hear them talk about the new gang residence that was going to be the deal site because the 4th amendment required a specific person and place to be searched. Cam did a quick drive by on the Meadow View Drive house and memorized a couple of plates. Both came back to known gang associates so he was sure he had the right location. He knew they wouldn't dare to use any of the obvious meeting houses because according to Lupe, J-Tra was absolutely sure they were under surveillance.

As Cam drafted the warrant he repeatedly called Mr. X "he" so as to throw off any heat from Lupe. He smiled at the thought that some gang member is likely to get hurt because these paranoid fools will want someone to blame. Whoever took over after the bust wouldn't rest till he found the person who talked. Since the facts described in the search warrant affidavit were detailed insider information it would only be logical that the snitch was high up in the organization. Disinformation wasn't just a tool used by government spies. Cops found it useful also.

Cam started to bring the sergeant and other gang team members in on the plan and Todd's partner Erin had already screened a home across from the target house for a cop-friendly place to establish a surveillance post on the crooks. She found a retired college teacher whose son in-law was a Monterey P. D. Officer, so that part was working well. All Cam really needed to do was finish the warrant and get a judge to sign it. Then, it was a wait till they arrive situation. The Sergeant's job would be to gather the manpower and have them ready for the raid when the time was right. The one thing Cam was sure of was that they would need a lot of cops because there were a lot of heavily armed crooks and the best way to stop a nasty fight was to overwhelm the crooks with officers. Make it look like suicide to fight. Police work is not a competition or sporting event that concerns itself with fair play. It's a business that relies on efficiency and effectiveness.

What Cam also knew deep down in his cop brain was that an operation like this was like setting a freight train in motion from the top of a huge mountain. Once it started rolling you lost control. Others would be involved making tactical and legal calls on a variety of issues. He knew he'd be a bystander once it started and it had already started.

∞

Bobby knew a few things also, and one of the things he knew was that Alex's next step would be to request, through official channels, Cam's time sheets and work schedules the day of the rescue. That was how any investigator would eliminate an alibi. When that happened, the cat would be out of the bag because all of administration would know that Cam was suspected of being the rogue cop who had done the cowboy rescue in the city of Mountain View, as Alex would have to explain his request. It won't happen instantly because Bobby knew a good investigator would nail down a bunch of other loose ends before he started to point fingers at another officer, but he knew he didn't have more than a couple of days to do something if he could figure out what.

Bobby's cop sixth sense told him that Cam had got the location of the house where he rescued the girls by some illegal means or he would have done it the right way and with a warrant. The only way he could think that Cam could have gotten that address is by beating the crap out of somebody and Cam would have had to find out which somebody. He was almost sure it was Ray who told Cam who to question. Ray and Cam had a pretty good relationship and he didn't think Lupe would have kept that from him. He needed to talk with Ray but first he needed to do some record checks and internet research. It was time to use his tech skills and crack this nut wide open to see what was on the inside. He also needed more information on who these girls were and how they were connected to Cam. He might even hack into the hospital records and see if they had any information about the girls.

ENGINES ALWAYS RUN FASTER JUST BEFORE THEY DIE

Cam didn't particularly like to talk on the phone but it did allow people a distance that was sometimes less stressful. He didn't want to force Jane into anything. He wasn't real sure what he was going to say but felt an urgency to repair his mistake.

He called her at work and said, "Hi, you got a minute to talk?"

She said, "Sure, what's up?"

He continued, "I'd like you to come to my house for dinner. Nick is heartbroken and misses you."

She couldn't believe this, "Really? Well, I miss him too. Are you going to be there?"

"Yes, I'm the cook."

She said, "Well, I guess that's alright. But it's him I really want to see."

Now what the hell does she mean by that? I guess a yes is better than a no. "Okay Jane, Friday at 7:00?"

"Okay, bye."

So far so good, but now he had to think about what to say and how much to tell her about his problem. He didn't want to jerk her around, but then he didn't want her to get away either. One of the byproducts of a personal crisis was it forced you to evaluate what is important in your life. After days and weeks of soul searching, he realized that his fear of commitment was borderline pathological and it was getting in the way of his happiness.

Think, Man! There's got to be a way to get through this mess.

∞

Bobby talked with Ray about the conversation he had with Cam and he had a quick look at the hospital's admitting records. He learned all he needed to know. It was Jimmy Scanlon's niece and the two pretty boys had been identified to Cam. Ray said one of them named Pedro had been laying low with a broken front tooth.

Bobby had to come up with a plan, but what? Cam had done the moral thing even if it was an illegal thing. A young girl's life was more important than legal procedures but the department and the courts wouldn't see it that way. God and Bobby would.

Bobby had a private place he liked to go to when he needed to think. No one knew about this habit of his, not even his wife. And he shared almost everything with her. His grandfather's grave site was in a sprawling cemetery on the north end of the city. He would grab a cold drink and sit on the lawn next to the grave. As he leaned up against a nearby Redwood tree he would talk with his grandfather and imagine the advice he would have given had he been alive. His grandfather took a particular liking to Bobby when he was very young, recognizing that Bobby was a unique, kind, and thoughtful kid. The advice Bobby received from him over the years was also spot on right and he often missed not being able to go to him after his death. Bobby told his grandfather everything that was on his mind about the situation with Cam's rescue and voiced all his fears and possible avenues of action. He sat there the better part of an hour explaining options and outcomes then he finally said, "Well Papa W, what would you do?" After about five minutes he stood up and said, "Okay, thanks."

The only way to fix this was to make the investigating officer, Mr. Alex Martinez, see it the right way. But how? If the decision on Cam's fate went any higher than the lead investigator, the politicians would decide and they were never brave. They were politically correct at all times because their professional future required it. Upward mobility had its price and the first installment was usually your ethics.

∞

J-Tra couldn't believe these cocksuckers he was dealing with. The connection for his dope was a big shot cartel lieutenant from Mexico who didn't trust anyone and wanted his cut of the money without losing sight of his dope. J-Tra didn't have the upfront money to get the dope because of all the grief the cops were giving him, so the deal was that the bikers would hand over the money and J-Tra would give it to the supplier before the dope left the house. That meant that there would be plenty of guns to make sure everybody did what they were supposed to do. The Bikers didn't want to pay right then, but J-Ta told them the supplier's conditions and that it had to be paid for COD. Both these assholes were talking about cutting him out of the deal and saving the middleman fee and they would too, if they knew each other well enough. To complicate things further, Manny Diaz wanted to be at the deal to make sure the big boys got their cut. It would be a miracle if he could get this thing to go down on time without anybody starting a shootout. All three of the guys he had to deal with were arrogant and had huge egos, especially Manny, so this deal was guaranteed to be difficult.

To top it all off the narcs and gang squad cops were breathing down his neck. His cell phone wasn't safe anymore and he had a rat on the inside somewhere. He just got a land line put in because he figured it would be harder to tap since the cops didn't know about this house and the phone was in his three-year-old nephew's name.

∞

When Bobby met with Ray he had been mining the internet for information and had a copy of a girl's picture he got from Facebook.

He blew it up and as he showed it to Ray he said, "Do you think $200 bucks would be enough to get you too friendly up to this girl?"

Ray said, "What?"

Then Bobby explained where this girl went to school and what her interests were. He knew her lunch period and what clubs she belonged to.

Ray said, "I don't go to that school and how am I going to meet her?"

Bobby told him, "Do you think they can tell one kid from another at a high school with a thousand kids? And all cafeterias are the same. You just go there during her lunch period say hello, introduce yourself and ask if she'd help you at the library. It's not that darn hard and if you can make it happen I'll give you another $300 on top of the $200. What have you got to lose?"

Ray asked, "What's the deal with this girl?"

Bobby said, "She got family that I'm interested in. I'll explain it all later."

Ray wanted to get enough money to buy a car. He was tired of all the hassles borrowing his sister's and this would go a long way toward that. The girl was cute but looked a little chubby so he might be able to get her interested in him. Most girls liked him so it wasn't out of the question.

"Okay, I'll try."

Bobby, knowing that teenagers had their own time schedule said, "I need this to happen, like now. Go to the school tomorrow. Right?"

Ray threw up both hands and said, "Yeah, okay, right."

Ray's family had it better than a lot of families in his neighborhood. They were poor, there was no question about that. But he had both a mom and a dad that hustled enough money to keep the family afloat. Dad worked in an auto body shop with a half dozen other illegal immigrants. Mom cleaned houses for rich women who all supported politicians who ranted about immigration laws. Ray didn't hang with the gang for money or status. He did it for protection. He and all kids his age got pressure from the various gang members to join. If they didn't the consequences were constant harassment and vandalism to their property. Occasionally if you got caught alone it meant an ass kicking. His plan was to make them believe that he was on board with the gang and slowly work his way away from them as he got older. He noticed that the gang didn't bother the older guys as much as the young ones and he felt that waiting them out and staying out of the heavy weight criminal behavior was the best way to survive. It occurred to him to ask for his dad's help but decided against telling him his problems because parents just didn't understand the situation. Calling the cops wasn't a solution; it was a way to get hurt.

∞

Ambrose thought a lunch with his old friend Lieutenant Jenkins was in order. He wasn't one of Jenkins's lifelong buddies but he did know him from local civic clubs and associations. He even represented Jenkins on a law suit. Jenkins got hit by a drunk driver a few years back, and the accident caused some minor injuries to Mrs. Jenkins as well as totaled a family car. Jenkins was so mad at the drunken businessman that hit him he hired Ambrose to make the guy's life a living hell, which he did.

The one thing Ambrose did know was that Jenkins was ambitious and was up for a promotion. He knew this because he made it his business to subtly interview every cop and law enforcement related employee that he had contact with. Intelligence is the lifeblood of an attorney's career. The more you know, the more you can influence outcomes.

Ambrose laid in a call to the Lieutenant and got the call back a few hours later. "Hi Raymond, how are things at SJPD?"

"Good, Ambrose and how are things in shark land?"

"Plenty of blood in the water, and we're doing well."

Jenkins smiled to himself and asked, "So what can I do for you?"

Ambrose replied, "Let me buy you lunch and we can discuss a few things. You wouldn't happen to be free today, would you?"

Jenkins said, "Ya, that will work." He and Ambrose set up a date for lunch and all the while the Lieutenant wondered what this slick old bastard had up his sleeve. He knew from years of following Ambrose's exploits that he was not a man to be taken lightly.

After Jenkins watched Ambrose eat more food than he thought humanly possible he tried to nail down exactly what this lunch meeting was all about. "So, Ambrose, why am I gifted with the pleasure of your company today?"

Ambrose wiped his mouth, pushed his plate away from his stomach and leaned back with a sigh. As he placed both hands across the expanse of his large middle he said, "I understand you're in line for a promotion soon?"

Jenkins thought, how does this guy know so much? It must be all these motor mouth young cops we hire these days.

"Yes, I'm on the short list for Captain, but these things are always unpredictable in the world of city politics."

Ambrose said, "Well, I'm not without some influence in certain circles. Perhaps I'll mention your name to a few councilmen that owe me a favor."

Jenkins could feel the slimy hand of corruption reaching up to grab what little independence he had left. "Why would you want to do that for me, Ambrose?"

Ambrose smiled and said, "I like people in high places to be reasonable and not be such self-absorbed prigs that they can't see common sense. I have come to know you as a practical man with a good deal of discretion. For example, this case that is rumored to involve a cop rescuing some girls from a life of prostitution. A simple man might pursue this with a mindless vigor that would result in a major shit storm that would impact everybody with long term consequences. Not that I'm the kind of guy who would instigate something like that, but, as they say, shit happens. You have the perspective of time and experience, particularly coming from the old days when things like this were handled in-house. You and I both know what justice is and what it isn't. I'm comfortable around guys like you, Raymond, because they're rooted in the real world. Do you mind if I make a few phone calls on your behalf?"

Jenkins thought about this for a few seconds and said, "Ambrose, I hear what you're saying and I appreciate your support but I can't make any promises. Situations like this tend to unfold on their own and not always the way we would prefer them to. I'm like most people. I deal with what I'm dealt."

Ambrose smiled and said, "I understand. Sometimes I'm dealt a hand where I can help someone and then sometimes I'm dealt a hand where I just have to fuck somebody over so bad it hurts."

Jenkins rose from the table and Ambrose followed. They dropped a pile of $20s on the table and walked out together. The cop in Jenkins was angry but the politician in him understood what had just happened. Ambrose was singling him out to apply pressure, but it wasn't personal, he was just doing his job. That's what he did for Jenkins when he got the fat settlement on the car accident law suit.

He'd have to look into this rescue thing a little deeper and see which way it was likely to fall. He didn't want to be on the wrong side of this case. It was obvious that there would be a major price to pay if he chose unwisely.

∞

Cam found himself contemplating his dinner date with Jane. She was independent beyond belief and sometimes hard to predict. She was the youngest of three daughters and very much like her mother. As a track athlete who specialized in sprinting and pole vaulting she was able to get several scholarships that helped pay for some of her college. She still worked out and ran and it showed. She studied in England to get her master's degree and was working for the police department just long enough to finish an administrative credential in education. Around the office she was known as "the ice queen" because she wouldn't flirt with the cops she worked with, but Cam knew she was anything but cold. He hoped she wasn't so pissed at him that she'd rip him a new one with what could be a dangerous tongue.

Jane looked great, she smelled great and she acted great. This evening was shaping up like it was all some giant torture exercise designed to drive him crazy. After she made a fuss over Nick and gave him a big bone to crunch she sat back and waited for the evening to come to her. Cam hated to be on the begging end of any relationship but he'd figured that he was about due to be on the other end of this game. They had a nice dinner of salmon, rice and salad with a pricey bottle of chardonnay while they played catch up on one another's life. It felt like she never was out of his life when they talked. She had a laugh that always made him smile. Since they'd been sitting for over an hour Cam asked her if she would like to go for a walk. It was good to get up and do something because his tension level was off the chart. He didn't know exactly what he was going to say or how she would react and he felt like his entire future depended on tonight.

So, they called Nick and took a slow hike under the canopy of large oak trees to a favorite granite outcropping where Cam liked to watch the city lights below.

When they were sitting down and comfortable, he said, "I've missed you and the only excuse I have for walking away is that I was scared. I like to be in control and I hate it when I'm weak. I guess I need to grow up a little. It's just that I've never felt this way about anybody before and it caused me to try to protect myself and not be vulnerable." Cam stayed quiet for a minute and stared off at the lights waiting for her to say something. He was afraid he was too late and that there had been too much damage done. He was waiting again for someone else to make the move.

Jane touched his arm and said, "You're really quite a nut job, you know. I've missed you too." She had the good tactical sense to stop there and let Cam decide how this conversation would unfold.

She was broken hearted when he'd cut off their relationship. She'd imagined a life with him complete with kids and travel and growing old together. She'd never completely given up on him but wasn't about to chase him because she knew that wouldn't work with Cam. She had dated a couple of times since breaking up with him but found herself comparing the guys to Cam and they just didn't measure up. A fact that pissed her off, mostly at Cam.

Cam tried to choose his words carefully but he knew he had to be honest because she was the one person in the world who could read him like an open book. Any bullshit and she'd walk.

"Jane, I'm involved in a bit of a legal problem right now and it's going to resolve itself in a couple of weeks one way or the other. If it goes bad I can see myself looking for a new line of work and I might possibly need dog care for a while. I want us to be together but I don't want to do it till I get through with this thing. I should have waited to talk to you till this crap was over but I figured I already waited too long and I didn't want to risk losing you to someone else. I don't know if you still want me and I hope I didn't screw this up."

She scratched Nick behind his ears and said, "Come on, it's getting cold." As they walked back to the house she didn't talk at all which really confused Cam. She did hold his hand and put her elbow inside his arm. He wasn't sure if she was cold or trying to be nice. When they got to the house she walked into the living room and started to undress as she walked toward the bedroom.

She was stepping out of her jeans when she said, "Why don't we talk about our plans in the morning. I've always loved coffee on the front porch here." As Cam followed her into the bedroom she finished taking off everything. She bent forward over the bed with her long dark hair falling to one side, flipped back the bed spread and slid into bed. In the moonlight shining through his large bank of bedroom windows he couldn't believe how naturally beautiful and uninhibited she was. He recognized at that moment, he was bagged, tagged, and caged and he didn't mind a bit.

∞

When Bobby called Ray to see how it went with the girl, Ray was more positive then he could have hoped for.

He said, "It went pretty good. I talked to some other girl in their group who was a big flirt but then got around to asking Angela about stuff I knew she was interested in. I chatted her up for a while and then asked her if maybe she'd help me with a term paper I was writing. She said yes, so we made a date to meet at the school library the next day after class."

Bobby told him to keep it up and that he was well on the way to payday. He also told him he might actually get some school work done too.

After a few days went by Bobby was pleased to hear from Ray that he was seeing Angela every day and that they seemed to be dating regularly. He laughed at himself because he was taking some pride in finding Ray a nice girl who was helping him get good grades.

∞

Now that Cam had his love life half way resolved he concentrated on getting this warrant finalized with all the extras. He was going to ask for a phone tap but the case law was making that a stretch so he decided that Erin's stake out operation would have to be the trip wire on this one. The fact that J-Tra got a phone in the name of a three-year-old cousin did help convince everybody he was up to something at this address. When Erin and her people saw activity at the house they would start to get everyone together. It was important that they be pre-briefed because once all the crooks showed up it would happen fast. As he and the judge were in chambers going over the warrant he had a moment that gave him pause.

The judge said, "Raise your right hand, do you solemnly swear that the foregoing is true to best of your knowledge?"

Cam crossed his toes and said, "I do." The judge signed it, told him to be careful and wished him luck.

Cam talked with Sergeant Glen and they went to the Lieutenant's office for a tactical evaluation. The Lieutenant said that because of the number of crooks involved and the potential for a shoot-out he was going to have SWAT stand-by for part of the take down. He wanted to keep the tactics fluid because he needed to use the heavy weight SWAT people where he thought a gun battle was most likely. They dismissed Cam after getting all the information he had and Glen and Jenkins cranked out an operation order.

Everyone was briefed in two separate meetings. Fifteen SWAT team members were put on standby and told not to leave the city and have their gear ready and waiting. They were given a location to respond to that was just a few blocks away from the target house on Meadow View Dr. One of the locations was a fire station which made it easy for the SWAT truck (more like a tank) to hide. The other was behind a commercial wholesale warehouse that had plenty of large dumpsters for concealment. They were told that they had to stay out of sight or the crook's counter surveillance would burn the whole deal.

SWAT had taken a lot of heat in the media lately because of the perceived "Militarization" of police but this is exactly the type of operation that benefits from the high force profile. Crooks of this caliber are heavily armed, unafraid of a shootout and violent beyond most people's understanding. An armored truck with flacked up tactical officers stopped violence by a show of force. It gave the impression that no resistance was possible.

The other briefing was a combined gang and narc squad affair. The target house was laid out in detail because Bobby had procured an architectural diagram of the floor plan from the city building and permit department. Some officers would be going in the house while others were assigned to take off any vehicles that had occupants. All the officers had raid vests that clearly identified them as law enforcement and hopefully would protect them from friendly fire. The Lieutenant knew that these deals seldom went down on time or in the way they were supposed to, so he planned an overkill with manpower so that if a few officers were out of contact he'd still have enough. He always had patrol if he needed it but that was a last resort because there were so many plain clothed cops involved it was dangerous to bring in officers who hadn't been briefed.

He admonished everyone, "Remember that every swinging dick out there has a police scanner so use the code sheet you've been provided and don't give out locations on the air."

Everyone waited. Erin was rotating narcs and gang squad officer through the stake out house. The college teacher who owned the place gave Erin the keys and told her to feed the dog, lock up when they were done and to call him when it was over. He went to Monterey for some peace and quiet.

Bobby had Ray and Lupe on alert to phone him if they saw anything that looked like it was a big deal about to go down. He cautioned them that J-Tra was watching everyone so they had to be careful.

Cam was sweating bullets because he'd called out all the special squads, cost the city a lot of money in overtime, guessed at a lot of unknowns and set a big stage for this raid. He would either be a hero or a fool. Time would tell which one it would be.

NOW!

When it went down it happened fast, but there was a slow waltz getting everybody into position, both crooks and cops. Dope dealers and thugs don't keep normal hours and they view showing up on time as a sign of weakness. They get up late and stay up late. The connection arrived two days after the bikers and the bikers were pissed because they didn't like waiting on a bunch of Mexicans and it was dangerous for them to sit around with that much money in a motel room. The advantage that gave the cops is that when multiple, greasy, hairy, white bikers were going to the Meadow View house it was a tip off to the surveillance team that the buyers were in town. They were followed back to their motel where a second surveillance was established. They stuck out like a red light because the neighborhood was lower middle class. There were a few cars on the street but most people there worked or went to school so adult men in groups were unusual. The narcs ran all the plates and used intelligence they gathered to confirm with Portland Police who all the players were. Portland even sent two of their narcs down to work with San Jose officers so they could add the information to their intelligence files.

When Ray called from his cell to tell Bobby that he thought it was happening because a bunch of the old timers were real active and a little edgy, Bobby told him to get away from the gang house and call him back. When Ray called back it was after 2:00 p.m. and Bobby laid a strange request on him. He asked him if he could call Angela on her cell and get her to go to the San Jose library with him to help him on a paper.

Ray said, "I guess so but why?"

Bobby said, "I just need you to do this and once you get her into the library tell her to turn off her cell because of library rules. She has to have her cell turned off. Borrow it if you have to and disable it. Leave yours on and I'll call you twice right in a row and when I do you bring her to an address I'll give you. You got that?"

Ray said, "Ya, I guess. I hope this is about over because this shit's getting kind of crazy."

"It's about over, Ray. If you can't get her to go with you, call me. Okay?"

"Okay."

Bobby was making a huge guess on timing but figured if it was a false call on the dope buy he really hadn't tipped his hand and could redo it later.

The two guys they had sitting on the biker motel about 30 minutes from the house called and said they had serious movement. It looked like three guys got in a brown Buick and six more into a blue Dodge van. The team said the van guys were carrying large duffle bags that looked like they could hold rifles or shotguns. Erin's team on the house said that they'd spotted cars leaving the house and driving around the neighborhood like they were looking for surveillance. All the teams were activated and were trickling into their assigned spots. The Lieutenant told Sergeant Glen that this baby was all his and that he should drive up to the stakeout house like he owned it, go in and give the signal when he thought it was time. Cam was already in the house and had parked his temporary ride, not the Mustang on a back street. He crawled a fence to get into the back of the house. Sergeant Glen assigned one half of the SWAT team to take off the van full of bikers and held half in reserve because he was sure that there would be a van full of Mexican dealers to take down. Everything was making sense. The bikers weren't going to walk into a house with a boat load of money because that was a sure-fire way of getting ripped. They'd send in the three guys to talk and look over the product. He guessed the Mexicans would do the same. They'd leave the majority of the dope in their vehicle until they saw some money. This is how this dance was done. Dealers and buyers walked around in circles trying to size up the other guy. It wasn't too much of a stretch to say it was like two male dogs sniffing each other's butts deciding if they should fight or not.

Erin cornered Sergeant Glen and Cam, "I want to hit Borracho with a probation search as this thing is going down. I think he'll be involved somehow because one of our units saw him leave the target house a while ago carrying a box. I'm not sure how but it's worth the effort."

Glen said, "We have a manpower problem Erin. We've tapped out the gang and narcotics operation."

Cam said, "Patrol can spring a few guys to handle it."

Sergeant Glen shrugged and said, "Okay Erin, it may be a little outside their expertise but see what you can put together."

"Thanks, Sarge."

Erin contacted a patrol sergeant she used to date who happened to be working this shift and explained her problem and what she needed done. She also told him she was concerned that with all the new rookies that they might miss some dope or investigative leads. He assured her that he would find the right people to hit Borracho's place. She had confidence in the Sergeant, he was a smart guy. She told him that when they made entry on the warrant she'd let him know so he could hit Borracho.

It had been almost an hour and a half since Bobby had talked with Ray and since he didn't get a call he hoped everything went down on Ray's end as planned. He sure wished he could check, but he guessed he'd have to just go on faith. This thing really looked like a go and he couldn't believe the Lieutenant and Sergeant would just walk away from this operation after all the time, people and resources they'd expended, so he laid a call into Alex Martinez. It took a while to get him because he was testifying in court and Bobby had to go through the bailiff to get to speak to him.

When Alex got on the line Bobby identified himself and said, "A bunch of us narcs, gang squad members and SWAT people are about to serve a warrant on a house in our city and I have reason to believe your daughter is with one of the gang members."

Alex was speechless and when he finally said something it was, "How do you know? Where is this?"

Bobby said, "Look, you try and call her on her cell and if she's in a house in San Jose tell her to calmly walk outside and walk away. If she doesn't answer, call me back and you can tag along on the raid. Here's my cell number." As Bobby gave him the number he could hear panic in Alex's breathing. He really felt bad about this because he had kids and this would be right up there with the worst call a parent could get.

Bobby got a call back in a couple of minutes and Alex was a basket case. Bobby told him to calm down and gave him a staging location where he and several squad members were waiting. He told Alex not to speed or draw attention to himself as he drove up or it could alert the crooks, which would endanger his daughter.

Alex drove up while the buyers and sellers were still doing their back and forth, looking at what each other brought to the deal and feeling out each other to make sure it wasn't a rip off. The Mexicans had driven up in a ¾ ton Chevy pickup with a cab over camper. The negotiators got out of the cab. The surveillance teams couldn't tell how many were in the rear but they did see considerable movement. The SWAT team sniper, upon setting up and using an infrared scope, reported at least four people in the back.

Bobby walked back to Alex when he arrived and shook his hand. He escorted him over to his car and handed him a tactical vest with "POLICE" across the front and back. Alex tried to find out how he knew all this information but he was afraid it was true because he knew there was a new boyfriend that she'd been phoning. She'd been secretive about him and Alex knew he didn't go to her school. He thought all the stories about going to the library must have been a lie which was new behavior for Angela but then she was a teenager. Bobby told him he'd fill him in later but essentially an informant was providing Bobby with information about the girl.

Bobby told Alex, "You need to stay with me when we make entry because no one knows you and you haven't been briefed."

Cam and Sergeant Glen watched as both the Mexicans and the bikers brought out a fairly large quantity of something in their respective bags. The crook's vehicles were parked about a hundred yards away from each other on the side of the street that the raid house was on. The bikers' Buick was empty because the occupants were in the house. This made SWAT's targets easy to deal with since it put some space between groups and both target vehicles were not directly in front of the house. Cross-fire was always an issue if shooting broke out.

At times like these innocent citizens living in adjacent houses were a big concern. Unfortunately, there was no way to get them out of the houses without burning the whole operation so the tactical commanders just tried to minimize their exposure and hope it went down without a firefight.

As the crooks all went into the front door of the house with what was suspected to be sample amounts of dope and money. Sergeant Glen said to Cam, "What do you think?"

Cam said, "I think that's good enough. We'll catch J-Tra with serious dope and the heavyweight guys are still in their vehicles, which makes it safer for SWAT. We really don't want this pack of heavily armed crooks spread out in this neighborhood with all these innocent civilians."

Sergeant Glen nodded and thought Cam showed pretty sound managerial judgment as he picked up the radio mic. And in his big booming baritone voice said, "All units this is the command post, you have a GO! Hit it now. GO GO GO!"

The SWAT teams and house entry teams all dropped their cars and trucks in gear and sped toward the house. The SWAT teams blocked in their respective targets with undercover cars and fanned out behind the cover of their armored vehicles. The team leaders were giving the crooks instructions over the loud speaker on how to surrender while the chemical agents' officers were loading and locking with a couple of burning grenades. They gave the crooks all of 20 seconds to surrender till they fired two hot canisters of gas into the camper and van. The SWAT commander decided that this situation was not going to be a prolonged negotiation standoff. This was followed by stun grenades. This particular little toy exploded with an eardrum shattering detonation and threw dozens of small rubber balls about the size of a marble at extreme velocity. They hurt like hell. The crooks would exit one way or the other because not only was this a huge amount of gas for such a little area but the burning gas grenades started fires. There were gas grenades that were blast type and didn't burn but they weren't very effective and the burning type were. Law Enforcement always told the press that there was no intent to start a fire but every commander who used the burning grenades knew that fire was the eventual outcome.

While all this was happening Cam, Bobby, Todd, Erin, Alex and 18 other officers were hitting every door the house had. They did a loud knock and notice at every door while the SWAT guys were surrounding their target vehicles and after waiting a few seconds to comply with "knock and notice" requirements they forced entry. The doors were blasted with a hand battering ram carried by two SWAT team members who were assigned the point on the house entry, then the raid teams went through the house cuffing everyone. The SWAT guys dropped their ram at the front door and joined the arrest team as they went through the house. Officers peeled off in partners and secured a room as the others leap frogged past them to the next room. This way they could secure the house quickly and not give the crooks time to escape, arm themselves or destroy evidence.

The trick on securing a house like this one was to move fast with lots of officers. If they had prisoners they would cuff them and drop them off in the living room just inside the front door where an arrest team would sit them on the floor and hold them till they could be transported to jail. The officers were all yelling, "Police-Search Warrant" so the crooks would know it was the cops and not another gang ripping them off. Occasionally a suspect would try to crawl out a window or run to a back door but they were grabbed by the collar or in the case of guys with no shirts on, by the hair and put on the ground to be secured. One fool was trying to put a big package of dope down a toilet and Todd kicked him in the ass so hard he flew behind the toilet tank and had to be pulled out by two other officers. He had a split forehead and two broken fingers to show for his efforts. The only deadly force used was in the master bedroom occupied by Manny and a whore.

Manny and Dory were lying in bed resting from a particularly violent episode of sex. Manny had a lot to drink and had been displaying his prison style of self-satisfaction. He learned as an inmate, sex is about dominance and submission and he'd never quite made the adjustment to being with a woman and being on the outside, so he treated Dory like he would a punk in the joint. She was bleeding from a cut lip and had a bruised throat where he had been squeezing her neck. She was just getting her breath back and touching a sore spot in her scalp where Manny had a fist full of her hair when they heard the cops announcing themselves at the front door. Manny knew that he could dodge any dope charges because he'd been in the bedroom for over an hour and didn't have any dope around him, but he couldn't beat the gun rap. As an excon in possession of a firearm he knew that it would cost him a return to prison and another strike under California's sentencing laws. As he sat on the edge of the bed he pulled the gun out of his pants that were piled by the side of the bed nearest the door and threw it to Dory.

"Bitch, you tell them that this is yours. Hide it in your clothes. If you don't, I swear I'll kill you." Dory picked up the .357 revolver that was favored by many gang members because it didn't leave spent brass at a crime scene like an autoloader would and pointed it at his back. If she shot Manny, she would go to prison but at least she wouldn't be raped and beat on every day. Her life was a disaster and she had nothing to lose. It simply couldn't get any worse. As the cops were outside the bedroom door screaming "Police-Search Warrant" and they kicked at the door to make entry she made a split-second decision. She pointed the gun over Manny's shoulder and squeezed the trigger twice. Her aim was at the top of the door because she didn't want to hit the cops on the other side. Manny, shocked by the detonation next to his ear, turned toward her and started to say something when she dropped the gun over his shoulder and it fell into his lap. She instantly dived to the floor putting the mattress and bed frame between her and any gun fire. Manny made the mistake of picking up the gun to give it back to Dory. At that moment two SWAT officers, armed with MP5 fully automatic machine guns kicked the door open and zipped Manny from his belly to his head with three rounds each. At his autopsy, the coroner would later comment on how the officers had stitched a perfect upside-down V in Manny.

One of the SWAT guys shouted down the hallway "Code 4" which meant everything was under control and they didn't need any help. They found Dory crying and beaten on the floor nearly under the bed frame but generally unharmed.

In a back room, two gang members were trying to get out a window when they were met with guns in their faces by officers stationed outside. Bobby and

Alex pulled the two thugs back inside. Bobby slapped a pair of cuffs on one guy and put him on his face on the floor.

He looked at the other thug all dressed in red and tatted up like a prison inmate with four dots under one eye and told Alex, "I think this is the guy that knows about your daughter." Bobby had never seen this gang member before but figured he'd do since he and Alex were alone in this back room with these two crooks. Alex was borderline crazy. The daughter he loved was in danger and this piece of shit held the answer to her location.

He stepped forward and pushed the thug against the wall. "Where is she?" The guy didn't say anything. "Where the fuck is she, my daughter?" The gang member just shrugged his shoulders and looked away like a tough guy who couldn't be bothered. Alex grabbed a hand full of hair and straightened the crook's head so that he was looking at him.

He crammed his semiautomatic gun barrel in the crook's mouth so far that it was up to the trigger guard and said, "I swear to God, I'll blow your fucking head off if you don't tell me where she is." The thug was scared and hurt because the front sight of Alex's autoloader was lodged against the roof of his mouth all the way to his throat. The look on Alex's face was pure rage and the only thing that kept him from pulling the trigger was his wanting to know what this punk knew about his daughter.

Bobby stepped in front of Alex and raised his hands. "Alex, calm down. She's not here. I'll call my informant and see where she is. Take the gun out of his mouth and breathe, man." Alex removed the gun and Bobby said, "Cuff him while I call my informant."

Bobby made the call as he stepped away from Alex and told Ray to come to a cross street near the raid house. He told him to stop at a corner nearby and call him.

"Alex, I called my CI and he's got your daughter. She's fine and he'll drop her off in a couple of minutes. She's fine man, relax."

Cam got to see the tail end of this performance as he walked down the hallway and wondered who the other cop was and what it was all about. He guessed he'd have to wait till things calmed down and he could ask Bobby.

Bobby felt extremely guilty over what he'd put Alex through, but on another level, he couldn't believe how well it had all turned out because, from his perspective, the investigating officer of his partner just engaged in the same activity as he was investigating Cam for and for the same reason. If that wasn't enough to give this guy some perspective nothing was.

All the crooks outside the house had surrendered without firing a shot. The bikers in the van were so cooked and gassed that they came out on their knees puking. The Mexicans were not in as bad of shape because they had the smarts to throw a blanket over the gas grenade, as well as some water as it burned, and they didn't eat as much gas. Major dope and weaponry was found in both vehicles and the charges looked solid.

J-Tra was caught with two pounds of meth at his feet and a .9mm Berretta in his waist band. He made the mistake of trying to run past Erin and he got a shotgun butt in the teeth for his trouble. Erin didn't pull her punch because she was venting a lot of anger over all the women victimized by this turd. J-Tra wound up on his ass with a bloody lip and two very loose teeth. Erin reached down and snatched his belt buckle knife while he was still seeing stars. An arrest team flipped him over and cuffed him before he cleared his head and assessed what had just happened. All of this made the Lieutenant and Sergeant very happy. Both were on a promotion list and this is the kind of case that seals the deal.

When Ray arrived with Angela, Bobby told him, "Ray drop her and drive away. I'll explain what's going on later." Ray just shook his confused head sideways and did what Bobby said. Alex seeing her on the street corner just north of the raid was so relieved to find her he hugged her and wouldn't let her go for five minutes. When Angela tried to find out what was going on and why her father was yelling at her about her new boyfriend it was like two different conversations. After a few minutes on the way home Alex calmed down and started to question his daughter like the true professional interrogator that he was. When he finally put it all together he realized what had been done to him. He was so mad he turned around to go get Bobby, then thought better of it because he had Angela with him. He made up his mind that he'd deal with those San Jose guys later. He swore to himself that he'd destroy the cops that pulled this shit if it was the last thing he ever did! Angela sat buckled in the passenger side of the car crying, still unsure what had transpired.

The total yield from the raid was more than 50 lbs. of meth. $575,000 dollars, 15 serious guns, 20 heavy duty arrests and one dead heavy weight excon named Manny. Not a bad day for the good guys.

Everyone was busy for the next five hours. Prisoners had to be booked. The Lieutenant had the District Attorney contact a judge for bail adjustments since it wouldn't do to let these guys get out on bail. Reports had to be filed and evidence logged. The logistics in securing the crime scene and all the equipment was another long job. By the time it was all done, everyone was bushed. They didn't have their normal post bust beer debriefing. Everyone just went home and went to bed.

Cam called Bobby the next day and said, "How' bout I pick you up and we swap a few stories."

Bobby said, "Sounds good, 9?"

"Okay, bye."

When Bobby got in the car Cam said, "You look sleepy. You want a sip of my coffee?"

Bobby smiled and said, "You never get tired of that one, do you?"

"So, tell me a story, Bobby. What was going on with you and that other cop in the house yesterday, and who was he anyway?"

Bobby knew it was time to come clean on his little deception. "He is the Mountain View investigator that was assigned to investigate the rescue of the two girls from the gang house. His name is Alex Martinez."

Cam was blown away. He looked at Bobby and said, "What?"

Bobby explained about meeting up with him at the gang investigator's meeting, Todd's comments and Bobby's subsequent fact-finding mission. He told Cam about having Ray get next to Alex's daughter and setting him up for some prisoner interrogation in the raid house.

Cam couldn't believe his ears. He pulled to the side of the road, parked the car and turned off the engine. This was not anything like the Bobby he knew.

He stared at Bobby in disbelief and said, "Aren't you afraid you'll go to hell for something like this, not to mention get fired?"

Bobby said, "Oh, I'll good with God, but I do worry about my job now and then. I guess I just have to blame my bad behavior on contamination from associating with you."

Cam was speechless because he was discovering an unfolding of events he never anticipated. "So, what did you and your new friend Alex do in that room at the raid."

"Well, I told Alex that the punk in there with us knew where his daughter was and the guy copped an attitude with him so Alex proceeded to feed him some gun barrel. All the way to the trigger guard."

"Where was his daughter?"

"She was with Ray. He took her to the library."

"Bobby, you're a fucking amazement. So, what's your plan from here? He has to have figured out by now what you did and my guess is he's madder than hell."

"Ya, I figured I'd let him cool down some and then see if he could be reasonable."

Cam was dumbfounded. He said, "Well, I guess I'll let you handle it because you two know each other and it would probably be best if I didn't talk with this guy. Ambrose would have my butt."

Bobby told him, "I plan on subtly telling him that you two are just alike and that it's very understandable. When someone you love is in immediate danger all the legal niceties are pretty irrelevant. I think he'll come to the same conclusion." As he started the car, Cam was shocked into silence. He couldn't believe after all his experience with Bobby that he'd do something like this. It was causing him to reevaluate everything he had taken for granted.

While Bobby and Cam were plowing through paperwork and waiting for other people to finish their pieces of this puzzle Erin was working hard on another angle. She had asked Bobby, Cam and Sergeant Glen to meet her in an empty conference room to update them.

"My probation search on J-Tra's brother Borracho went pretty well. My old boyfriend on D squad assigned Al "(I conceived him on duty)" Sylvester to lead the search and he did some shit that was amazing. They found a quarter kilo of dope at the house which was fronted to Borracho supposedly for testing. While they were there Sylvester did a sweep for stolen property and found a T.V. and computer that were stolen. Sylvester then had our IT guys crack the computer and found child porn. In other words, Borracho's one fucked duck. Al talked to the D.A. and was promised that they'd file charges on Borracho in adult court. Needless to say, he's scared to death. He just knows that if a chubby little punk like him goes to the joint for 10 years he'll get poked in his Australian eye all night long. So, Al made him an offer he couldn't refuse. He videotaped his full statement implicating J-Tra in the death of Dawn the prostitute and in return Borracho will be arraigned in juvenile court. Apparently Borracho loved Dawn as she was his first and he was mad as hell at J-Tra for ordering a punk by the name of Raphael to off her. The D.A. says J-Tra's homicide is a slam dunk case even if Borracho gets cold feet because the video statement is so good with tons of specific verifiable evidence that he's sure he'll nail him for 187pc. He's also sure he can play Raphael and J-Tra off of one another."

All three of the guys listening to Erin had a smile that was so big she was a little freaked out. Without saying a word Cam stood up grabbed her by the shoulders and planted a big kiss on her cheek.

Erin laughed and said, "You're welcome." She added, "Al Sylvester has put in for a transfer to the gang detail and I guess you guys know how I feel about that. He's got talent that we can really use." Sergeant Glen smiled and nodded thinking, there just might be a slot opening up.

∞

Alex went through a whole series of head trips, anger, relief, disbelief, frustration, and then anger again, then eventually acceptance. When he called Bobby to talk, Bobby recommended that they meet at a hamburger joint near the city limits.

Alex just studied Bobby for a while then said, "Okay, Officer Wright, why don't you tell me what the fuck this thing is all about, like I don't know anyway."

Bobby just nodded and said, "Look, first of all I'm really sorry about scaring you because I have kids too and that wasn't nice. It's just that I didn't know how else to get you to look at the situation from another perspective. At no time did I ever risk your daughter's safety. Ray's a good kid. You obviously can do anything you want but I'm hoping you'll look at the spirit of the law vs. the letter of the law. Remember that from the academy? Sometimes what's right gets confused with what's legal. Guys like you and I are so used to doing things by the numbers that we forget the human factor. My partner tends to be a little wild sometimes, but I've always admired his ability to look at things from a distance and make sure things turn out best for the people he's charged with caring for. He's taught me to reexamine my concept of doing the right thing."

Alex just thought for a while. This cop was good. He didn't pressure him. He explained everything without admitting anything. It's almost like he knew Alex was wearing a tape.

He pulled it out of his pocket, turned it off and sat it on the table in front of them. He said, "So you're saying your buddy Cam and I did the same thing?"

"No, Cam would never feed someone a gun barrel. He's much more subtle than that." Alex just looked down and sighed.

After what seemed like a long pause he asked, "What can you tell me about this guy Ray? Because it appears my daughter really likes him?"

"Ray's a good kid and he was a wannabe with the gang but those days are over. He wants away from them and now he's got to stay away from them because whoever takes over will be turning every rock to find out how things got back to the cops. He risked a lot working with us and he knew it was dangerous. He warned my partner about a guy who tried to kill him. But dating your daughter? That's another story. You'll have to make that call."

Alex said, "I have to go. To tell you the truth, I thought you were going to be a prick and I'm a little disappointed that you're not. I have to think about this whole thing for a while."

On the drive back to his city Alex ran through his options. He thought long and hard about all these crazy events of the last few weeks. There was no hurry on this decision. He needed to let emotion subside and not rush a conclusion or action. He also thought about his dad and "Another Village Pacified." He thought about his shooting of the mentally ill kid and he thought about doing the right thing, whatever the hell that was.

A week later Tom Grant from hospital security called Alex. "Hey, Alex, what do you want me to do with this security footage we were looking at? It's time to put it back in rotation and record over it or I could send it to you."

"Na, don't need it. That case went in another direction."

"Okay partner, talk at you later."

Alex tilted his chair back and said to nobody in particular, "Guess I made up my mind."

PUNISHMENT TIME

Lieutenant Jenkins called Sergeant Glen to his office for a private conversation about several sensitive topics. The raid results, the rescue, his promotion and the Sergeant promotion. All of these things seemed to be interrelated and interdependent. They could go positive like a well-timed symphony or negative like a chain reaction freeway pile-up. This was one of those pivotal moments in life when a small action had huge implications.

As Sergeant Glen was walking to Lieutenant Jenkins's office he was thinking to himself how the years had changed both Jenkins and himself. When they were young they had few thoughts about retirement, promotions, and politics. They kicked ass, took names and enjoyed just being cops. They'd have done it for free it was so much fun, but now they realized that their careers were in the last lap and that a comfortable retirement meant playing the game wisely. That was the major concern of the day.

"Hello, Raymond."

"Hi Bud, have a seat. I've got a few issues we need to clear up. Of course, all this is just between you and me."

"Sure, Lieutenant." Bud liked to call Raymond by his first name to remind him of their past together but thought calling him "Lieutenant" was a nice touch to show he respected his rank.

"Bud, these are sensitive times for both of us and a misstep could cause any aspirations we both have to be sent into oblivion. I'm getting feedback regarding the rumor of that rescue of the two girls from the gang house and it frankly has me worried. This is one of those situations where we either need to lay waste to whoever was involved or bury it so deep it never resurfaces. I'm looking for your input here because you're a little closer to the street than I am and probably have a better feel for how much of a problem this could be."

Sergeant Glen was not surprised by the cautious approach the Lieutenant was taking. He was a careful man these days, nothing like the man he was in his youth. He knew the Lieutenant wanted to be promoted to Captain more than anything right now and that he would do almost anything to make that happen.

"Well, Raymond, I've had my ear to the ground on this one for a while and I think I know the players."

Jenkins stopped him before he could say any more, "I don't think it's a good idea to name names at this point."

This was a huge road sign to Sergeant Glen. If Jenkins didn't want him to say the name then he was already embracing the defense of deniability, "I didn't know who did this."

Bud paused for a moment to get his thoughts and words together. "Raymond, a lot of these young cops are just like we were in the early days. Remember when you shot that body builder monster in the foot so you wouldn't have to fight him and wrote that report saying he went for something in his waist band." Bud started laughing and the Lieutenant smiled uneasily. Now that he had the Lieutenant in a less self-righteous state of mind he said, "I think this thing will go away. It's already dropped off the radar screen for most of the concerned parties. My understanding is that the other agency involved has stopped the investigation and that was the main threat. I would recommend we back off and do nothing unless it resurfaces."

Jenkins just nodded his head and said, "Ya, you may be right. I had lunch with our old friend, Ambrose, a while ago and he made it clear that he would start a major shit storm if it went forward. There was a time when a threat from a defense attorney would have pissed me off so much I'd have done the opposite of what he wanted in spite of the damage."

"I know the feeling, Raymond, but we're smarter now and we don't take things as personally." Bud thought to himself, that pretty much confirms that

Cam is our man if Ambrose is involved. He's a direct link with Jimmy Scallon and one of the kidnapped girl's last name was Scallon.

Lieutenant Jenkins said, "Okay, I agree with your assessment, but how do we control this loose cannon in the future. The successes he's had lately are only likely to encourage him to do more of this reckless shit. It makes me wonder about my decision to partner those two up."

Bud smiled and said, "We could neuter him the same way we were neutered."

Jenkins wasn't getting it and said, "What?"

Bud almost laughed and said, "Promote him. If we both move up there will be a Sergeant's opening. He's more than qualified, he's at the top of the Sergeant's promotion list and has shown excellent supervisorial judgment lately on a couple of serious incidents. Besides there's nothing like a little responsibility to make you behave with a bit more maturity. It worked on us."

Jenkins sat back in his chair, smiled and said, "It's good to see you're still the same old guy who glued all the Chief's desk drawers shut. Come on, I'll buy you some coffee and a piece of that banana cream pie you always liked."

∞

Alex saw Bobby about a month later as they were passing each other in court. Bobby stopped to say hello and shook Alex's hand. Alex said, "Tell your crazy-shit partner that I closed out that case due to lack of any evidence."

Bobby smiled at him and said, "My family is having a BBQ at Alum Rock Park Saturday. Why don't you grab your kids and come on out. No beer though, we're Mormons."

Alex stared at him for a moment and said, "Is it okay if Ray comes?"

Bobby smiled and said, "Sure."

The day was sunny and warm, and the BBQ food was delicious. As Bobby, Alex and Cam stood around waiting for some other family members to get all the kids split up into two softball teams they talked about the usual bitches all cops complain about.

As Cam looked out at all the kids being herded into two groups he told the other two guys, "One thing about having a picnic with a Mexican and a Mormon is you're guaranteed a full softball team."

Alex looked at Bobby and Bobby just directed two open hands toward Cam. "That's my partner." Jane having overheard the crack shook her head and lightly smacked Cam in the back of the head as she walked by.

Bobby laughed at a startled Cam and said, "So what are you going to do with that one?"

Cam shrugged and said, "Marry her, I guess. Any woman who says, 'We'll get through all of your problems and then make a good life for us and our kids,' is not someone you should let get away. Besides a Sergeant needs a wife for his image. Sergeant Glen got promoted to Lieutenant of narcotics and gangs, and they needed somebody to run the gang squad so, tell me congratulations Boys."

Bobby looked at Alex and said, "Good, we can use her help cleaning up after you." Alex nodded his agreement and Cam grinning, looked down at the ground and shrugged his shoulders.

ACKNOWLEDGMENTS

A writer needs victims to suffer with him. My friends, Dirk, Tony, Cisco and Air J. were there for me. Your time and advice are appreciated.

Cam, Bobby, Erin, Todd and Sgt. Glen, you know who you are and you're welcome for the name change.

ABOUT THE AUTHOR

Dale Hoagland is the grandson of a deputy sheriff who led his family to California's Central Valley during the Dust Bowl. He was lucky enough to have had a long and distinguished career in law enforcement.

Starting at age nineteen he worked as a correctional officer among hardened criminals in the prisons of Tuolumne County, before joining the Berkeley Police Department. As a rural valley kid working as a Berkeley rookie in the early 70s, he found himself chasing Black Panthers, fighting on riot lines and learning how to survive in a big city. He later became a narcotics officer in the rural communities of the Central Valley, where he joined a group of fellow narcs who experienced the drug wars of the 1970s from undercover and often from outside the lines of institutional authority.

Hoagland has an AA, BA, and MA in Police Science, Sociology and Criminology and has been a prison guard, police officer, deputy sheriff, state agent, and federal agent. His assignments have included narcotics, SWAT, hostage negotiations, range master, defensive tactics instructor, and detective. He held the rank of Narcotic Team Leader, Sergeant, and Lieutenant as well as Police Academy Director. He's a life time member of California Narcotics Officer Association and currently teaching in a law enforcement program.

He is also the author of *"Pig tales, a narc's story."* Available at Amazon Books.

PIG TALES

A NARC'S STORY

FROM THE BERKELEY RIOTS OF THE 70'S TO THE
CENTRAL VALLEY'S FIRST DRUG TASK FORCE –
THIS IS NOT YOUR TYPICAL COP STORY.

POLICE LINE DO NOT CROSS

DALE HOAGLAND

WHAT AMAZON CUSTOMERS ARE SAYING ABOUT HOAGLAND'S BOOK-

"PIG TALES, A NARC'S STORY"

Great sense of humor

I was a cop in Oakland when Dale was in Berkeley and the narrative is spot on. It will make you laugh! No embellishments of how great cops are and how devoted they are to duty, just an accurate picture of human nature on all sides of the fence. Great read. Couldn't put it down. The truth is stranger than fiction!

New found respect

Excellent story of an officer's point of view of the streets.

As a kid, I always wanted to be an officer. Growing up in a family from the other side of the tracks, I figured it was out of reach and just plain wrong. I grew up believing that these individuals were here to break up our families. After reading this book, it has given me a new-found respect for police officers and those individuals who risk their lives and livelihoods to protect all of us. Thanks to all who sacrifice their own existence to protect decency in the world. The world could be a better place if we all live in respect of each other

Best Cop Book Ever!

I have read many books on police work. This by far is the best! Great book, well written and keeps your attention. This book is a bunch of stories from "the good ole days." Police tactics have changed since the 1970's and 80's. When reading this tell all book please keep that in mind. Police Officers are good people who protect all of us. They are forced to do the job with an insane amount of rules. Criminals have no rules and often the deck is stacked in their favor. Anyone considering a career in Law Enforcement should read this book. Best book on police work ever!

Much Thanks

This book is so detailed, has you on the edge of your seat at times and it's hilarious. Thoroughly enjoyed reading this book.

Great book

This is the best book I have read. It's funny and very entertaining. I recommend this book to everyone. If you have a law enforcement background, it's even better.

A Good Read

It was a great read. Thanks for sharing your stories.

www.ingramcontent.com/pod-product-compliance
Lightning Source LLC
Chambersburg PA
CBHW050116280326
41933CB00010B/1122